ROMANTIC RECOLLECTIONS

MADAME LYDIA KYASHT AT THE PRESENT DAY, with her small daughter, Pouffée.

Frontispiece

ROMANTIC RECOLLECTIONS

By
MADAME LYDIA KYASHT

Edited by
ERICA BEALE

Noverre Press

First published in 1929

This facsimile reprint published in 2010 by
The Noverre Press
Southwold House
Isington Road
Binsted
Hampshire
GU34 4PH

© 2010 The Noverre Press

ISBN 978-1-906830-20-5

A CIP catalogue record for this book is available from the
British Library

PREFACE

How can anybody write a Preface to their own life ? It is a very similar task to attempt to write a Preface to one's Memoirs, but mine is really intended to give me the opportunity to express my most grateful thanks to those who have helped me to compile this book.

First of all, I must thank my friend, Miss Erica Beale, for her interest and labour of love in which she put all her heart and soul.

I want to express my appreciation also of the original manner in which Mr. Harry Folkard has arranged the illustrations. He has introduced a style hitherto confined to the illustrated pages of newspapers and magazines, and our thanks are due to him for his valuable aid.

I want also to express my sincere thanks to the following for assisting us by supplying material and data : to Mr. Arthur Aldin, the Manager of the Empire when I was dancing there ; to Mr. Fred Farren, the producer ; to Mr. Cuthbert Clarke, the musical director ; to Doctor Lennane for his assistance in research ; to Mr. L. A. Barbe for his photographic assistance ; and to Messrs. Maple for their courtesy in obtaining information from Mr. Shearburn, and in placing at our disposal the particulars of their contract for building the villa of the Grand Duke Boris.

In conclusion, let me add that if my life has been sometimes troubled, romance has helped to colour such trouble. I pity the man or the woman who has never heard the call of romance. They have never really lived.

Let us ring up the curtain on my " Romantic Recollections."

LYDIA KYASHT.

CONTENTS

CHAP.		PAGE
1.—Memories of my Childhood		13
2.—Russia of the 'Nineties		29
3.—Stories of the Emperor Alexander the Third		35
4.—My Girlhood		45
5.—Russian Court of the 'Nineties		53
6.—At the Wedding of the Ex-Queen of Greece		62
7.—My Confessions		70
8.—Sidelights on Russian Society		82
9.—Within the Palace of the Tsar		91
10.—Romantic Revelations		100
11.—A Sinister Figure		108
12.—My Own Romance		115
13.—Grand Dukes I have Known		122
14.—At the Villa of the Grand Duke Boris		134
15.—Stories of the First Revolution		141
16.—From Seven Pounds a Month to Forty Pounds a Week		149
17.—The Glories of the Old Empire Theatre		159
18.—Glamour of the Footlights		170
19.—My American Experiences		176
20.—Stories of King Edward and Queen Alexandra		186
21.—Celebrities I have Known		193
22.—Famous Beauties of the Past, and the Present		202
23.—Under the Red Flag!		210
24.—Stories of Kings and Queens I have Met		221
25.—My Escape from Russia		228
26.—Some Royal Romances		234

LIST OF ILLUSTRATIONS

1.—MADAME LYDIA KYASHT AT THE PRESENT DAY
Frontispiece

FACING PAGE

2.—PUPILS AT THE IMPERIAL BALLET SCHOOL - - 19
3.—MADAME LYDIA KYASHT IN ONE OF HER FAMOUS DANCING RÔLES - - - - - - 49
4.—ROLL CALL OF THE IMPERIAL GUARD - - - 57
5.—MY HUSBAND AS A PAGE TO THE TSAR - - 64
6.—IN MY GIRLHOOD - - - - - - 70
7.—TWO FAMOUS DANCERS - - - - - 103
8.—MY HUSBAND, COLONEL ALEXIS RAGOSIN - - 120
9.—PRINCE IGOR - - - - - - - 127
10.—THE INCOMPARABLE LYDIA - - - - 140
11.—WHEN BALLET WAS AT ITS HEIGHT - - - 154
12.—WHEN VARIETY REIGNED SUPREME - - - 163
13.—FAREWELL TO ENGLAND - - - - - 180
14.—THE EARL OF LONSDALE - - - - - 195
15.—A CHRISTENING - - - - - - 204
16.—A FAMOUS DANCER'S SON - - - - - 226

Romantic Recollections

CHAPTER 1

MEMORIES OF MY CHILDHOOD

Russian winters—Memories of my Fatherland—One method of combating the severe cold—The Volga—Russia in the 'nineties—Scarcity of newspapers—The first printing press at Moscow — A strange book — I am left an orphan — My sister-in-law beats me — My brother decides to have me trained as a Première Danseuse—The Imperial Russian Ballet School—A Court Institution—My first visit to a theatre — I pass my examination — My greatest treat — My secret ambition — I become a pupil instead at the Imperial Ballet School—Our three meat meals a day— Water is tabooed — My greatest friend — Tamara Karsavina—Those penitential week-ends — An opportunity for sly flirtation — Basis of Orthodox Greek Religion —The Holy Synod — Strange Sects — A Secret Sect — Horrible Rites — Our chaplain at the Imperial Ballet School — Father Basile's sweet tooth — I am confirmed— The Tsar's constitutional policy — Some ancient laws — An atrocious sentence — Why Peter the Great repealed one particular law — Another friend of mine — Karsavina and myself experience pride goes before a fall—What the boy pupils thought of our hair — My first meeting with Pavlova as a mimic, and as friend.

I WAS born in Petrograd, or St. Petersburg, as it was then called, and was the only daughter. My parents had three sons besides, George, Nicholas, and Serge, but the last-named died when he was still quite an infant.

With the exception of myself and my brother George, none of the family took up dancing professionally.

My recollections of my life in Russia as a child are best described as a series of somewhat blurred pictures. When I close my eyes I can conjure up a vision of snow, of women muffled to the ears in furs, and of men similarly muffled who tramped about in massive Wellington-shaped boots. The memory of those boots, and the sound of the " tramp, tramp," of them on the hard frozen ground still lingers with me after all these years. The Russian winter used to be a very long and severe one, and we frequently experienced intense frosts as late in the year as May.

Agriculture was never at a high level in Russia. When I was a child, the landed proprietors were always complaining of their impoverished condition and lack of capital, and saying how impossible it was for them to pay the higher wages demanded by the peasants. The peasants, on the other hand, displayed a lively discontent with their lot. They declared they preferred to work in factories rather than accept employment as agricultural labourers.

When my father was not too absorbed in business affairs, he used to tell me stories about the emancipation of the serfs in 1861, which he, in turn, had heard from *his* father. He always declared that their change of conduct could be traced to this Act. Certainly it was true that after 1861, numbers of peasants forsook their fatherland and emigrated to foreign countries.

During the Russian winter a great many of the poorer children never stirred outside their homes, owing to the bitter cold which prevailed everywhere ; and in order to keep them warm their parents used to sew them into their garments. One doubts whether such a practice would meet with approval from disciples of the daily *cold* bath, but in its defence one must urge that those Spartan individuals, in all probability, have never experienced in their lives such intense cold as was endured throughout the Russian winter, and cannot appreciate the suffering which it entailed.

During one winter the Volga remained frozen for more than five months. This gives an idea of the time the cold weather lasted.

My recollections of my childish impressions of my country are as indistinct as my impressions of its climate. Looking back I seem to remember it as a vast land of impenetrable forests, interspersed by marshes and lakes, and rolling stretches of green prairie.

In the 'nineties Russia was still very behind the times in many of its ways and customs. For example, St. Petersburg had only six daily newspapers, while the remainder of the vast Russian empire was supplied with a meagre daily service of about thirty-three. It is hardly surprising that, under such conditions, the peasants remained ignorant and illiterate.

It was not until nearly eighty years after William Caxton had introduced printing into England, that the first printing press was established at Moscow. It was directed by two Russians, Ivon Feodorov and Peter Timofieiov ; and even after that the progress of printing was so slow that the first Russian book was not published until 1564 —eleven years later, to be exact. This was entitled the *Apostel*, and contained the Acts of the Apostles, and the Epistles.

On the whole, book publishing does not appear to have received any greater encouragement in Russia than that accorded the newspapers; for up to the year 1660 only sixteen books altogether were printed and issued by a rival printing firm.

My father told me about a curious book published during the reign of Ivan the Terrible, and which was known as the Domostroy, or Book of Household Management. Its authorship was attributed to a monk named Sylvester, who had written it with the intention of presenting it to his son and daughter-in-law. Sylvester held views on matrimony which were the reverse of saintly, since the main theme of his book centred around the supreme authority of the husband, and set forth the latter's right to inflict whatever chastisement he pleased upon the wife of his bosom.

When I was seven years old my mother died, and as my father did not survive her long, my guardianship devolved upon my brother, George. He was married, so I went to live with him and his wife. I had always been fond of George. In fact he was the only grown-up person, apart from my father, for whom I cherished any deep affection, for I can remember very little about my mother. And although my father adored me, my chief recollection of him is being deeply occupied with business affairs or suffering from spells of ill-health.

I cannot truthfully declare that I was devotedly attached to my sister-in-law, but neither was she to me. On the contrary, she used to beat me frequently with a little birch cane, which is called a *rosgy* in Russian. I can still recollect the painful stinging sensation, and how it made me feel as if my bare body had been rubbed over with a bunch of stinging nettles. No doubt I was a very tiresome little girl, but most of my so-called bad behaviour was due to high spirits rather than real naughtiness, only my sister-in-law could not, or would not, realize this, and never made allowances.

When I was a child my emotions were more indefinite than crystallized. I cannot remember hating anybody, even my sister-in-law, but I think this was because I was too superficial in those days to experience any kind of violent emotion.

My brother was a *Premier Danseur*, and possibly this accounted for his desire to try to get me into the School of the Imperial Russian Ballet as a pupil.

It was considered a great honour to be admitted a pupil of the Imperial Russian Ballet School, as it was a Court Institution, and maintained by the State. And apart from that, its general standard of education was very high. The main object of the teachers was to develop the brains and intelligence of their pupils. Although it was primarily supposed to be a School of Dancing, only a short part of the day was devoted to studying that art, and the rest of the time was occupied with classes on literature, science, and the general curriculum of an advanced college.

Until pupils reached the age of seventeen and a half they remained in the School, but after that age they were admitted to the Imperial Russian Ballet.

As the Imperial Russian Ballet was a Court Institution, the general procedure adopted at its performances was quite different from that adopted at any ordinary theatre. On Sundays and alternate Wednesdays, only subscribers were admitted, and on these occasions all the élite of Russian society were to be met there. The ticket system was unique, as the seats were handed down from one generation to another; with the result that some members of the audience boasted they had never missed a single performance in forty years.

I was seven when I went to a theatre for the first time. I was taken to see a performance of the ballet given in the Tsar's private theatre, at the Red Village (called *Tsarskoe Selo* in Russian). It was a great honour to be invited to a performance there, and child though I was, I was very proud about it. I am afraid that I cannot recollect the name of the ballet which was produced that evening, but I know the whole performance made a deep impression on me.

After my eighth birthday my brother George decided it was time to try to get me into the Imperial Ballet School, and arrangements were made for me to go up for a preliminary examination. When the day arrived, my sister-in-law dressed me in a blue frock, trimmed with cream lace, which had puffed sleeves, a low neck, and a huge bow at the back of the waist. I loved this creation, and thought myself very smart indeed. Ever since I have regarded blue as my lucky colour, for I passed my examination and was chosen out of several hundred.

George was determined to make me a *Première Danseuse*. He was very displeased with me when

PUPILS AT THE IMPERIAL BALLET SCHOOL.

Sitting, from left to right: Lopokova (sister of famous dancer), Lydia Kyasht, Polakova, Karsavina. *Standing, from left to right*: Chernithsky, Feodorovna, Proudnikova.

Facing page 19

MEMORIES OF MY CHILDHOOD

I expressed a wish to become a laundress instead. Such was my childish ambition, and my greatest treat was to be allowed to wash my dolls' clothes.

I had a large family of about a hundred dolls, which I tolerated only because of the pleasure it gave me to launder their garments. None of them were very big, but that was not surprising since the average cost of each was about twopence. I made a chemise for each doll, and as I carefully washed and ironed it daily, it will be understood that my weekly wash was a heavy one. In my nursery there was a complete laundry in miniature, including an ironing board and a variety of tubs and irons. When I entered the Imperial Ballet School, my principal regret was that I was obliged to leave my precious washing apparatus behind. I shed bitter tears over the thought that there would be nobody to wash my dolls' chemises, and the prospect of becoming a famous dancer in the future, which my brother dangled before my eyes, did not compensate me in the least for his refusal to let me become a professional laundress.

Pupils were very well fed at the Imperial Ballet School. This was not the case in the ordinary Russian schools, where pupils were sometimes under-nourished. But in our Imperial School we were, if anything, over-fed. If you look at the photograph on the opposite page you will see that we look very buxom maidens to be prospective *ballerinas*, and not in the least like the ethereal beings that popular imagination pictures such persons to be. This was not to be wondered at since we had no fewer than three solid meat meals a day. Our breakfast was the only meatless meal. This was served at nine o'clock, and consisted of milk and bread-and-butter.

At one o'clock a two-course luncheon of meat and sweets was served. Veal, stewed in the most appetizing sauce, was a favourite dish, and so were cutlets. At five o'clock we all sat down to a three-course dinner of soup, and meat or game, and sweets, and at eight o'clock another meal was served, which was called supper. At this meat again formed the staple dish. This was our last meal of the day, and we used to do full justice to it. To tell the truth, we were greedy little creatures; and we experienced no difficulty in complying with the strict rule of the Imperial School that we must leave nothing on our plates. The only time when I found it difficult to obey this order was when fish was on the menu. I hated fish! As a child my favourite food was a sort of minced cutlet, served and cooked in the Russian manner, and whenever this was on the menu it was a red letter day for me.

Nobody drank water as a beverage in Russia. The national drink for school-girls was cider, or *kvass*, as it is called in Russian, and very delicious it is too. We used to drink it for luncheon and dinner, but at supper we had tea or milk instead.

Looking back it puzzles me to know how we children managed to eat the amount of food we did, without ruining both our complexions and our digestions for ever. However we contrived to do so, and none of us seem any the worse to-day, either from a Terpsichorean or digestive point of view.

MEMORIES OF MY CHILDHOOD 21

One of my greatest friends at the Imperial Ballet School was Tamara Karsavina, who was destined to make her name as a *Première Danseuse*. We played together and we took our punishments together, for both of us were mischievous children and full of high spirits, although in justice to Tamara I must admit that I was usually the ringleader in our pranks, while she was an obedient lieutenant. I am afraid I must have been a thorn in the side of my teachers, for I was no sooner out of one scrape than I was in another. They used to punish me by keeping me at school during the week-ends, instead of letting me go home.

During these penitential week-ends my teachers compelled me to attend the services held in the Imperial Chapel, but this was not really such a punishment to me as they fondly imagined, for I enjoyed the services, not so much, I fear, from the amount of religious instruction which I received, but on account of the opportunity which it gave me to indulge in a little mild flirtation with fellow pupils of the opposite sex. Even at that tender age I was not averse to flirting, and as I was obliged to curb my desires in this direction during week-days (it was a strict rule that girl pupils should not converse with the boy pupils, and if anybody was found transgressing this particular order, severe punishment followed swiftly), I looked forward to my penitential week-ends, because of the opportunities it gave of eluding the eye of authority, and talking to the boys.

The pupils of the Imperial Ballet School belonged to the Orthodox Greek Church, the State religion, of which the Tsar was the head. The

Holy Synod was its supreme organ. This had been established in 1721, and was presided over by a lay Procurator, who represented the Emperor and exercised very wide powers in ecclesiastical matters, although the actual making and annulling of appointments rested in the hands of the Tsar alone.

The very basis of the Orthodox Greek religion is that the Church is by Christ's ordinance unalterable, and that its traditional forms were established in the beginning by Christ and His apostles, and must neither be added to nor altered. In 1654 when Bishop Paul of Colomna boldly disagreed with certain changes approved by the Holy Synod, he was deposed from office, taken captive, and was beaten and flung into prison, where he remained until he went raving mad, and died.

The Russian peasant used at one time to be somewhat pagan in his general outlook, and indeed displayed a preference for keeping upon good terms with the pagan divinities. In the seventeenth century various schisms occurred. One of the most powerful sects were the Bezpopovtsi, while the most extraordinary were the Molchalyniki, or mutes, the members of which, as their name suggests, were not permitted to utter a word, and had to remain silent under torture even. Closely akin to these were certain mystic sects, of whom the most remarkable was the Khlysti. This sect came into existence as far back as 1645, when, according to their belief, God the Father descended in a chariot of fire upon Mount Gorodim, in the province of Vladimir, and took up His abode in the earthly body of a peasant, Daniel

MEMORIES OF MY CHILDHOOD 23

Philippov. The latter selected a fellow-peasant, Ivan Suslov, to be his son, the Christ, and Suslov in turn selected a "Mother of God," and twelve apostles. Suslov was a remarkable character altogether, for although he was twice crucified, and also by the Tsar's orders beaten until the skin was flayed from his body, he survived and did not die until seventy years afterwards.

Before his death he chose as his successor another peasant, Prokopiy Lupkin, and since then, according to the belief of the Khlysti sect, every successive generation has had its divine Christ, and its "Mother of God," who are worshipped because of the Divine Spirit that dwells in them. According to the twelve commandments issued by their founder, Daniel Philippov, alcoholic drink, marriage, and so-called fleshly sins, are all prohibited. Dancing is not banned however, providing it is of a certain character. It forms a feature of their prayer meetings, when to the accompaniment of the chanting of hymns the Khlysti performs a Dervish kind of dance, which gradually becomes wilder and wilder, until the dancers finally drop upon the ground exhausted, and, foaming at the mouth, begin to prophesy. The most remarkable thing about this particular sect, however, is that it is a secret one, and that its members belong ostensibly to the Orthodox Greek Church.

The Skoptsi was a much more horrible sect. It was really an offshoot of the Khlysti, but its followers, with the idea of obtaining salvation, practised self-mutilation, and even went so far as to cut off their women's breasts. This horrible sect was founded in the latter part of the eighteenth century by a man called Selivanov, and seems to have had a morbid attraction for many people. Despite the repeated efforts of the Government to stamp it out, it still persisted.

Religious instruction formed an important part of our scholastic education at the Imperial Ballet School. Our chaplain was a delightful and very handsome old priest named Father Basile. Our priests are not required to remain celibates, and so Father Basile was married, and had a large family of about ten children. He had one weakness, a fondness for sweetmeats, which we children were quick to turn to our personal advantage. Knowing this trait of his, we made a habit of saving the sweetmeats given us at dinner and supper. We used to pool our store, and when the time arrived for our Scripture class would present our combined offerings to the good Father, and innocently plead to be told a story in exchange. Father Basile was a talented story-teller, and we children used to take it in turn to stimulate his imagination with sweetmeats, whenever he showed any signs of flagging. The result of this strategy on our part was that the Scripture hour would often pass without our receiving any religious instruction at all. Poor Father Basile used to be very distressed when this happened, and I can see him now shaking an admonishing forefinger at us, and calling us " hardened little sinners ! "

Confirmation takes place at an early age in our church, and I was only eight years old when Father Basile prepared me for mine. Even now I can recollect the surge of solemn emotion that overwhelmed me, and how my childish sins swelled to enormous proportions until I felt buried beneath their weight. I shall never forget either the sense of relief that stole over me, and the utter comfort that succeeded my first confession. Easter is kept as a great festival in Russia, and so our confirmation took place during Lent. Everybody fasted, and none of us were allowed to eat any meat, or to drink any milk. On the Friday we had to keep our fast unbroken, until our first confession had been made to the priest.

In my childhood the constitutional policy pursued by the Tsar was that of suppression, and it was this policy that probably sowed the seeds of the subsequent revolution. As far as the law and its administration was concerned, it had certainly progressed in some ways since the reign of the second representative of the House of Romanoff, the Emperor Alexius, but the progress was extremely slow. This monarch is famous for having established the *Ulozhenie*, or Ordinance, whose principal objective appeared to be the championing of brutality in every conceivable form. One of the most popular punishments recommended by the *Ulozhenie* was to bury alive any married woman who had been found guilty of the offence of murdering her husband. Presumably, if the situation were reversed, and the husband was found guilty of murdering his wife, nothing would have happened to him, as no mention was made of his fate. According to *Ulozhenie* law, it was legal to torture anybody in order to extract evidence, while the use of the knout was freely advised, and mutilation was recommended.

Some of the penalties set forth under this latter heading would have been absurd if they had not been so atrocious. For instance, if a man ventured to smoke tobacco, the *Ulozhenie* law decreed that he should be punished by having his nose cut off. This particular law was repealed by Peter the Great when he ascended the throne, because he enjoyed smoking himself, and so could hardly condemn his subjects for following the Imperial example.

I have already explained my friendship with Karsavina. Her brother was also a great friend of mine. Now he is a famous professor of philosophy in Petrograd. He was exceptionally clever as a boy, and when I failed in any particular examination, which was a not infrequent occurrence, he would take me in hand, and although he was only four years older than myself, coached me during the week-ends, which I spent at their home.

Karsavina and myself were rather vain, and took a great pride in our personal appearance. Both of us were very unhappy because we had such sparse heads of hair, if not the scantiest in the whole school, as we admitted to ourselves with shame. The affliction was the greater in our eyes because it was the fashion for pupils to have luxuriant heads of hair, and to wear it in two plaits, tied at the ends with black ribbon. The boy pupils used to admire this style, and so we had to suffer the added mortification of watching them admiring the thick tresses of our feminine rivals, until the pair of us could have wept with rage and mortification.

For a long time we did not know what to do to alter this state of affairs, until at length we conceived the idea of collecting the combings of our fellow-pupils. As far as colour was concerned, it was a somewhat mixed " bag," but by dint of carefully sorting, and of dividing the fair from the dark, we eventually contrived to collect sufficient combings to make into four plaits. We fixed these false plaits in our own genuine, but scanty, locks, and tied them up with black ribbon. The finished result was so successful that nobody could tell by a cursory glance which was false hair and which was real. All went well and we revelled in the admiring comments of the boys about our beautiful heads of hair, until one of the teachers, unable to restrain her surprise at seeing me appear with long hair instead of my usual scanty pigtail, inquired the reason for this sudden transformation. And being of a suspicious disposition she gave my plaits a tug.

My precious combings came away in her hand and left me with two tiny pigtails, which were utterly useless to attract the boys. Karsavina did her best to console me over my loss, but my vanity was sorely hurt, and took some time to recover.

Another famous dancer who was a fellow-pupil with me at the Imperial Ballet School was Pavlova. She was older, however, and therefore in the senior class to myself. The juniors regarded the seniors as beings set apart. Various privileges were accorded the latter, one being the possession of a private study. I shall always remember my first meeting with Pavlova. It was on a day when I had been kept in as a punishment for over-bold conduct. Boldness seemed to be the favourite definition given by my teachers to my conduct, although I think such a term was unduly harsh. On this particular occasion I was the only pupil undergoing a spell of detention, and so had the large empty classroom to myself. Very forlorn indeed I felt as I sat there, and viewed the world in general, and the Imperial Russian Ballet in particular, through most jaundiced eyes.

Just then Pavlova came into my classroom, and taking pity on my forlorn and solitary state, invited me to accompany her to her study. Instantly I was transported to the realms of delight, for to me she had always seemed to be a species of goddess, and so it was an absolute miracle in my childish eyes that such a being should condescend to notice my existence. I followed her in a state of beatitude that rendered any expression of gratitude impossible.

Pavlova is a very clever mimic, and she proceeded to entertain me and the other seniors gathered in her study by giving us a realistic imitation of some of the male ballet dancers in the Imperial Opera House. At any other time I should have been delighted at the prospect of meeting some of the seniors who were gathered there, but Pavlova's personality wholly overshadowed them, as it has overshadowed so many since her formal *début*, and I watched her spellbound, aware, in my childish mind, that I was in the presence of someone who was a genius in her art.

Throughout my career Pavlova has shown me great kindness, and when I made my first professional appearance she personally introduced me to the audience, and presented me with a beautiful bouquet of red roses. Among real artistes professional jealousy does not exist. Instead there is a spirit of camaraderie and a genuine desire to pilot a newcomer towards success.

CHAPTER 2

RUSSIA OF THE 'NINETIES

How the dynasty of the Tsars was founded—A policy of suppression—The Prince who was thrown to the hounds—The beginning of serfdom—Secret Police—A spy—A new terror—The Kuryadniki—To Siberia—Russian folklore—A legend—An interpretation of the three crows of a cock—The most popular Russian legend—The reign of despotism—The real characteristics of the Moujik—A similarity to working classes of other lands—Glittering Russia of the 'nineties—The reverse side of the picture.

To understand the composition of the Russian character one has to go back many centuries to the period of Independent Principalities. There is a legend to the effect that this dynasty was founded by three brothers, who were hardy Norsemen. Their names were Rurik, Sineus, and Truvor, and from their dynasty sprang the Tsardom that was destined ultimately to wreck Russia.

When Ivan the Great abolished the system of Independent Principalities and became the first Tsar in 1462, he adopted the policy of suppression that was to be such a feature of future Imperial Rulers. He imprisoned and beheaded his unfortunate nobles upon the most paltry excuses, and it was said of him: " That no Sovereign in Europe was so well obeyed." His precepts were duly imbibed and practised by his grandson, Ivan the Terrible, who during his minority, when still only a boy of thirteen, asserted his authority by accusing some of the nobles of robbing the

Treasury, and ordered the leader, Prince Shuiski, to be torn to pieces by a pack of hounds as a warning to his followers.

It was not this Emperor who created serfdom, however, but the brother-in-law of his son, a Russian noble called Boris Godunov, who having got himself elected Tsar, proceeded to institute certain reforms, one of the first being the inauguration of a state of serfdom. In justice to him, it must be urged that the cultivation of the country had been so neglected, through inability to obtain adequate labourers, that it became a vital necessity to introduce some system to amend such a state of affairs. Some estate owners treated their peasants fairly, and did not take advantage of the situation, but some adopted quite an opposite policy, and exacted everything they could. The peasants were supposed to work out the payment for their allotments by personal labour, or else by a money payment, but if an owner were so minded, he could enforce conditions that prevented the wretched peasant from ever attaining complete ownership of his strip of land. Such authority did the estate owners possess that they were at liberty to inflict what corporal punishment they pleased upon their peasants, and it was not until many years afterwards, in 1904, that this licence was revoked by law.

To add to the terror of the peasants there was the all-powerful Secret Police, called the *Ohrannoie Otdelenie* (*Ohranka*), renamed *Tcheka* by the Bolshevists (now called the *Ogpu*), and before which, in later centuries, even the most rabid revolutionists were destined to tremble. At one time the police used to provide a porter, or *dvornik*, to work at the big buildings and houses. He was really a spy, and received instructions to report any suspicious incident or any seditious speeches immediately. This unfortunate man was obliged to remain at his post for sixteen hours at a time, and was not allowed to sleep or to rest at all while on duty.

On the plea of preserving order throughout the rural districts, the Tsar Alexander the Second added a fresh terror to those already endured by the overburdened peasantry, by creating a force of mounted policemen. These received instructions to patrol the country districts, and to arrest summarily anyone who aroused their suspicions. The peasants speedily nicknamed them Kuryadniki, or chicken-stealers, as poachers appeared to form the bulk of the prisoners.

It was not safe for anyone to attempt to take the part of the peasants. An author named Alexander Radistchev attempted to do so, and wrote a graphic description of the miserable conditions of the serfs during the reign of Catharine the Great. He was punished for his temerity by banishment to Siberia.

Folklore has always abounded in Russia, and some of the legends have been handed down in verbal form from one generation to another, as the people heard them sung originally by strolling minstrels. There were many legends woven around the period of Ivan the Terrible, and one in particular relates in vivid imagery the story of his death. As a child I loved listening to legends. One of my favourites was called "Christ and the Geese." It related how one day Christ and Saint Peter were out walking together, and Saint Peter said, "How fine it must be to be God. If for half a day I might be God, then let me be Peter for the rest of my days."

On hearing this wish expressed, the Lord smiled, and answered:

"Your wish shall be granted. Be God until nightfall."

The legend went on to tell how Saint Peter arrived at a neighbouring village where a Feast Day was being celebrated, and found a peasant maiden abandoning a flock of geese in a meadow. When he reproved her for this callous action, she told him: "It is a Feast Day, and God Almighty will look after the geese in my absence."

Since Saint Peter was deputizing for God, he was obliged to remain in the meadow and safeguard the geese until nightfall. The legend added that the Saint was very angry, and that he never again wished to be God.

Another legend which appealed to me as a child was one called "The Sun, and how it was made by Divine Will." It began: "The sun is thirty times the size it appears, because it is very high from the earth." An Imperial note was given to this particular legend by the statement that the "sun had a crown which would benefit a Tsar, and that God had consigned one hundred angels to enrobe the sun in apparel, and a crown made for a Tsar." To this legend may be traced the meaning attached to the three crows of a cock, as it explains how, when a cock awakens, he flutters his wings, and crows in order to announce the resurrection to the world, and that his second crow means "O Christ! Giver of Light! Look down on us, and bestow Thy light on the world," while his third and last crow is interpreted as being, "Christ is the Life, and accomplishes all things."

This quaint legend ended with the explanation: "Thus the cock sings to the Light, magnifies his Creator, and announces Joy to the Just. Amen."

The most popular of all Russian legends is the one, probably the best known of all, which relates the story of Prince Igor. The original manuscript was at one time carefully preserved in a monastery at Yaroslavl, but was burnt in the great fire at Moscow. Fortunately a transcript of it was found among the papers of the Empress Catharine.

Already in the Russia of the 'nineties there were to be glimpsed signs of the discontent smouldering beneath the surface, but the absolute despotism of the Imperialistic group was unchallenged. Although the peasants were freed from serfdom they did not find any great pleasure in their freedom, and were now grumbling that the Government was squeezing the last opek (Russian penny) from them by means of taxation. The *Moujik*, or Russian peasant, has been accused of many things, including laziness, ignorance, and that he has the "mind of a hog." In reality he is, in the majority of cases, a simple-hearted fellow. It is true that when his passions are aroused he becomes a beast, but otherwise he is a simple, friendly-disposed soul, who merely asks to be permitted to live in peace and quietude with his family. He bears one resemblance to the working classes of other countries in that he cherishes a pathetic belief in the ability of the Government to repeal taxation, and to provide him with work and a home, and implicitly believes that the Party who promise him such amenities will fulfil them. But such faith as this is not confined only to Russians. It may be encountered in Hyde Park on a Sunday morning, amid the crowd who listen to the tub-thumpers, or in New York, or in any of the capitals of Europe.

I cannot speak from personal recollection of Russia of the 'nineties, because I was too young to remember it, but my father engraved upon my childish mind a vision of St. Petersburg as it was then, peopled with officers in glittering uniforms, and lovely women bedecked with jewels; of the Imperial Opera House on a Gala Night, and the brilliant Court functions held by the Emperor Alexander the Third, when the Winter Palace was a blaze of colour and light.

My father showed me also the reverse side of the picture, of the peasants labouring without adequate reward, and groaning under oppressive taxation, and with hate smouldering within their breasts, ready to blaze into fury at the first spark.

CHAPTER 3

STORIES OF THE EMPEROR ALEXANDER THE THIRD

The seeds of Nihilism—Bombing the Palace—What saved the Imperial Family?—An unlucky number—A dastardly manifesto—The effect upon Alexander the Third—An Emperor who hated Jews—Victims of supreme autocracy—Queen Victoria's opinion of the Tsar—The Empress Marie Feodorvna—I am disillusioned—Characteristics of the Empress—The Tsar Alexander the Third—His wonderful memory—When I danced before His Imperial Majesty—An irate producer—I am accused of spoiling the ballet—The Grand Duke Vladimir—A nickname—The Grand Duke Constantine Constantovitch as a playwright—How the Imperial Pages were chosen—At the Alexander the Second Cadets' School—The Tsar visits the Cadets' School—An impromptu escort of five hundred cadets—The death and funeral of the Tsar Alexander the Third.

THE Tsar Alexander the Third succeeded his father Alexander the Second in 1881. The reason of his sudden accession—due to the assassination of his father by Nihilists—made a profound impression on his character, and was largely responsible for determining his method of government. It caused in him a reaction against any reforms that promised a greater freedom for the people.

Nihilism originated during the reign of Alexander the Second, and it was Ivan Turgeniev who first made use of the expression in one of his novels. He wrote of a new type of modern youth who dressed in slovenly fashion, and allowed his hair to grow long and straggling, who openly reviled the conventions. The young women, on the contrary, according to Turgeniev, must have been the pioneers of the Eton-cropped damsels of to-day, for they clipped their hair as short as they possibly could. The policy advocated by these youthful firebrands was the ever popular and perennial one of equal distribution of wealth and the abolition of the landed proprietor, and they preached this doctrine to the peasants on every possible occasion. Their favourite and most widely used argument was that " A shoemaker who distinguishes himself at his trade is a greater man than a Shakespeare or a Goethe, because humanity needs shoes more than it needs poetry." Naturally this sort of argument went down very well indeed with the ignorant peasants who, like the majority of people, enjoyed thinking of themselves as embryo geniuses thwarted by circumstances. Turgeniev christened these young would-be reformers Nihilists, much to their disgust, since they regarded themselves as potential saviours of their Fatherland.

In 1866 their pernicious doctrines began to bear fruit, for an attempt was made to assassinate the Emperor Alexander the Second. It failed, but that did not deter the Nihilists from making other attempts during the next fifteen years. On one occasion a bomb exploded inside the dining-room at the Winter Palace in St. Petersburg, and the Imperial family owed their lives solely to the fact of their being a few moments late for dinner! The members of the Imperial Suite were not so fortunate. Ten of them were killed and thirty-four other persons were wounded in this particular explosion.

People who associate ill-luck with the number

EMPEROR ALEXANDER THE THIRD

thirteen will regard it as a further proof of the truth behind this superstition that the Emperor Alexander the Second should have been assassinated by the Nihilists on March 13th, 1881. He had been reviewing a military parade, and as he drove back to the Winter Palace a Nihilist threw a bomb at him. The explosion mortally wounded the Tsar, and he died shortly afterwards. The Nihilists were very proud of their bloodthirsty deed, and on the following day the leaders issued a manifesto, setting forth that their " Secret Tribunal had condemned the Tsar to death, after two years of effort to bring about the deed."

The assassination of his father made Alexander the Third very bitter against the revolutionaries, and he took active steps to limit their power for the future. Six years later they attempted to assassinate him, but the attempt ended in complete failure, and the arrest of all the parties concerned. The Tsar did not confine his suspicions to the Nihilists alone. He insisted that Bismarck was planning a secret campaign against Russia, and therefore refused to renew the Treaty of Skierniewice when it expired in 1887, but made overtures instead for an alliance with France. He also began a severe campaign against the Jews, and went so far as to restrict their choice of employment and of residence. It is possible that he may have inherited some of his hatred of the Jews from his grandfather, Nicholas the First, who used to say : " It was my English nurse, Miss Lyon, who first inculcated me with a wholesome hatred of the Jewish race."

The Tsar Nicholas the First frankly loathed them, and on one occasion, when he was sentencing a Jew *to ten thousand strokes*, said : " *Thank God, we have no capital punishment in Russia.*"

This remark shows how a continual policy of despotism and suppression will end by killing all sparks of humanity in an individual. I imagine this particular victim would have welcomed hanging as a merciful fate in comparison with the one which he received.

Mingled with my childish memories is yet another picture, of a vast stretch of snow, its white purity stained here and there by ominous crimson patches, a grim testimony of the spilt blood of those unfortunate victims of supreme autocracy.

Yet there was another side of this Imperial autocrat, for when Queen Victoria spoke of the Emperor to a mutual friend, Her Majesty said : " He feels kindness deeply, and his love for his wife and children, *and for all children, is very great.*" Whether his subsequent conduct disillusioned the Queen, or not, one cannot say, but on another occasion she was less flattering in her description of him, and declared : " I do not think him very clever. His mind is an uncivilized one, and his education has been neglected. . . ." Then, apparently relenting somewhat, and fearing her criticism had been unduly harsh, Her Majesty added the rider : " He is bald, but in his Chevalier Garde uniform he is still magnificent, and very striking."

Such was the grandfather from whom Alexander the Third inherited certain characteristics, and whose grandson, the Grand Duke Michael Mikhailovitch, contracted a morganatic marriage with the Countess Torby.

EMPEROR ALEXANDER THE THIRD

The Empress Marie Feodorvna, Alexander the Third's consort, was a Danish Princess, and a sister of Queen Alexandra. She embraced the Orthodox Greek Church upon her marriage, and was a keen upholder of its traditions. I remember being terribly disillusioned by my first glimpse of the Empress. Childlike I had expected her to wear a golden crown, and the sight of her minus this Imperial ornament disappointed me bitterly. It was some time before I could be consoled. The Empress was always very kind and gracious to the pupils of the Imperial Ballet, and when we performed in the Private Theatre at the Winter Palace, or at the Marininskoe Theatre, St. Petersburg, would reward us with boxes of chocolates and sweets.

Her Imperial Majesty had the most beautiful hands I have ever seen. They were so soft, and most delicately perfumed. We children regarded it as a special treat when we were allowed to kiss them, and we would surreptitiously inhale the fragrance of her delicious perfume as we did so. I have never smelt any perfume like it since, and my memories of the Empress Marie Feodorvna will always be associated with the exquisite garden-like fragrance that seemed to be wafted with every movement she made. When she died in 1928, although she had left Russia nine years previously, there was a general feeling of grief throughout the Fatherland. She was a woman of remarkable energy, and she expended it in helping her husband and later her son, the Tsar Nicholas the Second, who was destined to be the last of the reigning House of Romanoff.

It is difficult for outsiders to realize what an

important part ballet dancing played at the Imperial Court, but in Russia dancing has always been regarded as one of the supreme arts, if not the foremost. The Empress Marie Feodorvna took an active interest in the education of the younger generation, and especially in the pupils of the Imperial Ballet.

Discipline was so strict there, that if any of us failed to pass our examinations we were punished by having our holidays stopped. French was the principal spoken language, as this was the one most in use at the Imperial Court, and the result was we all spoke it fluently. The Imperial Ballet School was managed by a Board of Control, consisting of eight women members elected from the teaching staff. As the appointment was a Government one, and the post carried with it various valuable emoluments, such as a residence and a pension after twenty years, keen competition ensued whenever a vacancy occurred. Madame Lihoscherstova was the head of the Board of Control, and was accorded extra privileges. She was allotted a marvellous flat in the Imperial School, as well as a carriage and pair, and a staff of servants. Small wonder that the highest in the land used to compete for the privilege of serving upon the Board of Control of the Imperial Ballet School.

The Tsar Alexander the Third also took an active interest in the Imperial Russian Ballet, and in the pupils of the Imperial School, and we used to perform before him every Sunday. When the performance was over he would summon us to the Royal Box, and talk to us, and in all sorts of ways he showed himself cognisant of intimate

EMPEROR ALEXANDER THE THIRD 41

details concerning our lives. He had a wonderful memory, and would disconcert us by reminding us of answers we had given on previous occasions to his questions, and which we had forgotten. When he had finished speaking to us he used to dismiss us with a smile and a gift of chocolates. We thought him a very striking-looking man, and admired his big red beard, and Imperial moustache of the same fiery colour.

I remember dancing before Alexander the Third when I was quite small. A special ballet called " The Caprice of a Butterfly " was being performed, and to my infinite pride and delight the producer, Leon Ivanoff, gave me and Karsavina two parts in it. Some of the child pupils of the Imperial Ballet School were to represent different insects in the ballet, such as grasshoppers, fireflies, and caterpillars. Ivanoff cast Karsavina and me for the rôle of caterpillars.

I was ambitious to give a really realistic performance of this insect, and thus impress the Tsar with my ability, so I practised in private all the contortions which I associated with a caterpillar, and, not content with giving a solo performance, persuaded Karsavina to join and copy my example. When the ballet was performed Karsavina and I writhed and wriggled, and generally behaved as if in the last stages of internal agony. Ivanoff viewed our efforts with such disapproval that he told us we had ruined the ballet, and brusquely ordered the pair of us off the stage. In fact, it very nearly proved to be my last performance.

I am afraid that I did not take the lesson as much to heart as I should have done though, and instead held obstinately to the opinion that

Ivanoff was jealous of my performance, which was certainly a piece of vanity worthy of a better cause. We were never told what the Emperor thought of our behaviour, but since he always upheld the tradition of the ballet, it is to be supposed he did not see much humour in our conduct.

The Grand Duke Vladimir, a brother of the Emperor Alexander, was a great favourite with the pupils of the Imperial Ballet School, but mainly for the material reason that when he visited the school he always begged a few days' holiday for us. This action completely won our hearts, and made his visits more than welcome.

The Grand Duke Vladimir had married a German Princess, the Grand Duchess Marie Pavlovna of Mecklenburg-Schwerin. She was very popular, and it was largely owing to her undoubted charm as a hostess that her husband became recognized as one of the leaders of Russian society in St. Petersburg. His daughter, the Grand Duchess Hélène, is to-day the Ex-Queen of Greece, and her wedding was the first State ceremony which my husband attended in his capacity as an Imperial page. I have danced many times before her father, the Grand Duke Vladimir, and also before the Grand Duke Constantine Constantovitch, a cousin of Alexander the Third. The latter Grand Duke was well over six feet in height, and had ginger-coloured hair. My husband has similar-coloured hair, and he has told me since how the Prince bestowed the nickname of "Rougée" on him in consequence.

The Grand Duke Constantine was a very clever playwright, although his talent in this direction was not widely known to the general public. A private performance was given in the Tsar's own theatre at the Winter Palace of one play which he wrote called "Judas." It was set to music, and those who were fortunate enough to see it spoke highly of the play, but as Christ appeared in the cast the authorities refused to grant permission for a public performance. At the performance in the Palace all the parts were taken by well-known society people, and the Grand Duke Constantine himself played the lead. The Tsar and the Imperial family were present, and invitations were confined to the immediate Royal circle.

Although my husband was one of the pages at the period of which I am writing, he was still training at the Alexander the Second Cadets' School. Only sons of noblemen were honoured by appointments as Imperial pages, and their names were put forward immediately after their birth. When they reached the age of nine or ten, those who wished to do so could join the Cadet School. They usually remained there until they were about thirteen or fourteen, and were then transferred to His Imperial Majesty's Page School.

There were great preparations whenever the Emperor paid a visit to the Cadets' School, and new blankets were even brought out of storage and placed on every bed. A concert was always held in the School Hall, at which an orchestra composed entirely of cadets formed the principal feature. And after an Imperial visit the cadets were given three days' holiday.

I remember my husband telling me how, after one visit of the Tsar, about five hundred cadets surrounded his sleigh and formed themselves into an impromptu escort to convey him to his palace.

When Alexander the Third died the cadets were chosen to form a guard along the Nevsky Prospect (Avenue) for the funeral procession. It was winter and the snow was lying thick on the ground. The funeral procession was so long that it took five hours to pass, and some of the cadets collapsed through being nearly frozen to death. During the period that the Emperor lay in state, every town sent a representative to pay homage at the Imperial bier, and it was a most impressive spectacle to see them all filing past.

The death of the Emperor made a deep impression on my childish mind. My father was driving me to school in a drosky, and as we drove along, I noticed groups of weeping people standing about in the streets. I could not understand what they were crying about, but when we reached the school we found the building closed and a printed notice fastened on the door informing us that " Alexander the Third is dead."

CHAPTER 4

MY GIRLHOOD

How Russian girls were chaperoned—My own quintette of chaperons—My first grown-up party—General Gelabuski—My only experience of drinking champagne—I mistake it for kvass (cider) with dire results—Maurice Petipa, the Maître de Ballet—A most obstinate man—Paul Gerdht—A platonic favourite of a Tsar—Madame Sokoloff—Her unhappy marriage and its romantic sequel—Her one fear—A shock—Karsavina and I leave the Imperial Ballet School—An engagement at the Imperial Opera House—The most miserable experience of my life—An alarming adventure—Karsavina and I are nearly drowned—A depressing sequel from our point of view.

WHEN I was a girl, chaperonage in Russia outdid even Victorian standards of strictness. Young girls of noble birth were never allowed out of doors by themselves, and always had some older person in attendance. This surveillance continued until they reached the age of twenty-one, when it was relaxed. Presumably their elders held the opinion that the fact that the girls had attained their majority meant that they simultaneously attained to an age of discretion as well! A girl who did not belong to such exclusive circles was not quite so rigidly chaperoned, although, according to the standard of the younger generation of to-day, it would have seemed very strict.

As for me, I have always been a law unto myself in certain matters, and chose to be the same in this case. My admirers acted in the capacity of chaperons, and as there were never fewer than four or five of them, nobody could complain that

I lacked surveillance. Whether such a procedure was correct is perhaps open to question, but I do know that my quintette made the most charming and tactful of chaperons, and that I loved each of them.

It was the custom in Russia for young girls to put up their hair at a much earlier age than was the case with English girls of that period. I was only sixteen when I put mine up for good. It sounds curious to modern ears to use the term " putting up the hair," but then one must remember that those were not the times of shingled heads, and that a woman's hair was still considered to be her " crowning glory."

I shall never forget my first grown-up party, not only because it was such a momentous event to me, but also because it was my first and only experience of drinking champagne. My host was General Gelabuski, the Minister of Transport, and he had issued invitations to a large party at a fashionable Moscow hotel. My brother escorted me to it. I was tremendously excited at the prospect, and delighted with my new evening frock, and the way the hairdresser had dressed my hair high on the crown of my head.

From my childhood I had been accustomed to drinking the Russian *kvass* (cider), so when somebody offered me a glass of sparkling golden-coloured wine, I drank it off quite unsuspectingly, thinking it was my favourite *kvass*, whereas it was champagne. The Russian champagne is quite different in taste from the champagne served in England. It is much sweeter, I am told, as the Russians detest sour wine, and will not touch it if they can avoid so doing. There was some excuse

MY GIRLHOOD

therefore for my not recognizing any strangeness in the flavour. Anyway, feeling particularly thirsty I drank off a tumblerful of the sparkling beverage, and finding it to my liking asked for a second, and then a third! My recollections of the party after that are extremely hazy. I do remember being violently sick, but the rest is oblivion.

When I was at the Imperial Ballet School, Maurice Petipa was the Maître de Ballet, and had held that position for sixty-five years. Petipa had the reputation of being a most obstinate man. I think this originated probably through his stubborn refusal to learn to speak the Russian language, as despite his many years' residence in the country he could only count up to the figure eight when I knew him. He was eighty-nine when he died, but remained quite active to the end. The Tsar thought so highly of him that he appointed him Soloist to His Majesty. Only three other artists were similarly honoured by the Tsar, among them being Madame Dolina, the famous contralto, who had been on the stage for thirty years.

My teacher, Paul Gerdht, was the chief mime artist at the Imperial Ballet School. He was a German by birth, and such a handsome man that all his pupils, myself included, fell violently in love with him. It has always been one of my pet theories that love acts as a mental stimulant, and it is a fact that all Gerdht's pupils were successful in their subsequent careers, which supports my contention.

I also studied under Madame Sokoloff. She was a remarkable woman altogether, and had enjoyed the unique position of having been a platonic favourite of the Tsar Alexander the Second. So highly indeed did this Emperor esteem her, that he even granted her permission to wed a naval officer. This action roused considerable comment in St. Petersburg, as it was a generally accepted rule that no dancers of the Imperial Ballet School were allowed to wed either an officer of the Imperial Navy or of the Imperial Army, unless the reigning Tsar chose to grant a special dispensation in their favour, and it was seldom that any Emperor exercised this Imperial prerogative. Unfortunately for Madame Sokoloff, her marriage did not turn out a success, and within a year she fell madly in love with a wealthy German, Edward Goer. After a while her husband divorced her, and her subsequent romance with her lover I will refer to later.

Madame Sokoloff was a brave woman in every respect but one. She had an inordinate fear of horses. Whether her mother had been frightened by one before her birth, I cannot say, but the mere approach of a horse was sufficient to throw Madame Sokoloff into an absolute panic. I remember what a fright she gave me once when we were driving together in a sleigh. The sleighs were built low on the ground, and if a horse were near, and felt a desire for human companionship, he could gratify that wish by resting his head on the shoulder of the nearest occupier of the vehicle. Madame Sokoloff and I had large fleecy shawls wrapped round our heads to protect us from the biting cold, but these also acted as a hindrance to any intelligible conversation.

Suddenly I noticed that our horse was using

Madame Lydia Kyasht in one of her famous dancing rôles, and (*inset*) as she appeared for her first professional performance at the Imperial Opera House at St. Petersburg, when she was only eighteen.

Madame Sokoloff's shoulder as a resting-place for his head. She remained entirely oblivious, thinking that I was the weary culprit, and while I did my best to persuade the horse to choose another place, she carried on an animated conversation with me in the most unconcerned manner. This abruptly ceased when, happening to turn her head, she perceived the nearness of her four-legged neighbour. I thought the shock had killed her, it took me so long to bring her round.

I was not really happy when I was a girl although I was so mischievous and full of pranks. In fact, I think the latter were more often intended and made as a challenge to fate than anything else. When Karsavina and I were sixteen and a half we left the Imperial Ballet School and accepted our first professional engagements. As a rule pupils remained at the Imperial Ballet School until they were over seventeen, as I have previously explained, but in the case of Karsavina and myself our teachers admitted that we showed exceptional talent, and so the rule was rescinded in our favour.

I obtained an engagement at the Imperial Opera House. In those days dancing was the greatest joy of my existence, and the photograph on the opposite page shows me as I looked at eighteen, when I was first launched on my career as a *première ballerina*.

I think the most miserable experience of my life was one associated with my girlhood, when I was suffering from a severe attack of diphtheria. I was taken away from the Imperial Ballet School and sent to the isolation hospital. We pupils had always enjoyed the rare occasions when we were indisposed and sent to the school infirmary.

This was a very luxurious place, and patients were allowed the privilege of ordering what food they fancied. We all made the most of this particular concession, so one can imagine what a shock it was to me to be transplanted from such comfortable surroundings as these to a bare-looking hospital ward. But the worst part of all was the total lack of privacy, and the close proximity of the other patients, some of whom were dying. The fact that a screen prevented me from seeing them was no hindrance to my active imagination, and I lay in bed and shuddered from head to foot with mingled fright and alarm. After a while, when the nurses learnt from where I came, they moved me into a small private room, adjacent to the general ward. But I shall never forget the torments I suffered at first. It made an impression on me that nothing will efface.

Karsavina and I had a most alarming experience together once, in the course of which the pair of us were nearly drowned. In our girlhood we used to spend the summer holidays at a small place near Pskov. It was a very favourite spot with artists, and had become a sort of artistic colony where everybody knew one another, and behaved as if they were an immense family party.

One day a number of them arranged to visit a neighbouring lake and picnic there, and as Karsavina and I had been disobedient, it was decided to leave us behind as a punishment. We felt very ill-treated as we watched all the others going off, and determined to be revenged.

After giving the matter our gravest consideration we came to the conclusion that the best revenge would be for us to go for a row on the lake, and join them later. We knew that this was a flagrant transgression of the rules, as we received the strictest injunctions never to row on the lake unless we were accompanied by an older and responsible person, but that knowledge only made our action more thrilling. We got into a boat and commenced rowing, but Karsavina was not so expert as I, and experienced difficulty in manipulating her oars. This difficulty increased when we approached the centre of the lake where the ripples began to assume a resemblance to waves. This upset Karsavina's oarsmanship altogether, and she lost her oars which drifted swiftly beyond our reach. Then, to add to our troubles, a storm sprang up and it began to lighten and thunder in an alarming fashion.

Karsavina was a religious-minded girl, so I begged her to pray for our safety, thinking the act would help to allay her own fright. In response to my suggestion she knelt upright in the boat, and prayed with great ardour, while I put forth the whole of my physical strength meanwhile in rowing our small craft into smoother waters. In the end some peasants on the shore saw our plight and rescued us both from a watery grave.

One would have imagined that after such a strenuous experience our chief thought would have been to get home as speedily as possible, but instead we went on to join the picnic party.

To our delight, when we arrived there, nobody asked us how we had come, and nothing was said until the party was on the verge of breaking up, when a question arose as to who should take us home. We then found ourselves obliged to confess we had come alone and unaided.

The sequel to this particular adventure was a painful one, as on our way back we encountered Karsavina's father, and a search-party dragging the lake for our bodies. Unluckily for us both, his joy at our safe return did not prevent him from impressing the lesson of our misdeeds on us by means of a severe whipping.

From that time dates my grudge against the prodigal son, and my suspicions concerning the absolute veracity of his story, and of the welcome extended to him.

CHAPTER 5

RUSSIAN COURT OF THE 'NINETIES

In the Palace of the Emperor Paul—A weak Tsar—How the Order of the Knights of Malta was founded—At the Imperial Page School—Camer Pages—Memories of the King of Siam—Baron Frederiks and his nephew—A quaint Court post—The Skorohod—The Tsar's chef—Recollections of the Tsar—An Imperial gardener—Choosing the Ladies-in-Waiting—In the Pages' School—The Roll Call of the Pages—Discipline in the Pages' School—Reporting for leave of absence—A lengthy formality—A novel signal—Off duty—An amusing incident and an impromptu bath—Those skin-tight breeches—An " accident " that befell one Imperial page—The Grand Duke Constantine Constantovitch sees the joke.

ALTHOUGH externally the Russian Court appeared to be very moral, such morality lay on the surface and one never knew what was going on behind the scenes. My husband, Alexis, has often told me stories of the time when he was a pupil at His Imperial Majesty's Page School, and also about the period when he was acting as a page at the Imperial Court. To give some idea of the state of affairs which existed it should be said that boys of fourteen were men of the world in experience.

I have already explained how the Imperial pages were chosen. When they left the Alexander the Second Cadets at the age of fourteen, they were transferred to His Majesty's Page School. This was situated in the palace that had formerly been the property of the Emperor Paul, a son of Catharine the Great. This particular Tsar seems to have been chiefly noted for his weak character, for, although he obviously desired to undo some of the actions of his Imperial mother, his impulsive efforts merely resulted in still further dislocating affairs, and failed to produce any beneficial effect at all. In his character he displayed that supreme autocracy which has been such a feature of the Russian rulers, and sought to model himself on Napoleon, just as his father, the Emperor Peter the Third, had modelled his actions and policy on Frederick the Great.

Such a policy ended, as might have been foreseen, in the assassination of the Emperor Paul, and although an outward show of grief was displayed, the nation did not really mourn in their hearts the loss of a monarch who had utterly failed to hold either their trust or their respect.

The Emperor Paul had taken an active interest in the Order of the Knights of Malta. This ancient order was formed at the time of the Crusades, with the object of protecting the Christians in the East against the infidels. After they made their headquarters at Malta, Napoleon seized the opportunity, on his way through to Egypt, to attempt to disperse them. When the Emperor Paul heard of this he immediately offered them his Imperial protection; so the Knights of Malta took up their residence in his palace, and it was afterwards converted into the Imperial Page School.

Pupils attached to this school were divided into two sections, the Junior and the Senior. There were about one hundred and fifty pupils altogether, of whom about thirty belonged to the Senior division. The great ambition of any boy in this division was to become a Camer Page, because the first Camer Page was given the appointment of Page to the Emperor, and the second and third Camer Pages were appointed to the Empress, and the fourth and fifth to the Dowager Empress. When my husband was at this school the King of Siam was a Page. He was accompanied by a friend of his, Prince Nai-Pum. One of them acted as a page to the Tsar, while the other was attached to the Tsarina. Although they were princes of the blood royal neither of them received any different treatment from that meted out to the other Pages, and both were always addressed by their Christian names.

When the King of Siam left Russia later to return to his own country the Tsar presented him with a gift of two magnificent white horses.

" I have never seen such horses since," declared my husband. " There was not one single speck of colour to mar their spotless whiteness, and their coats gleamed like satin."

Everybody was sorry to bid farewell to the King of Siam and Prince Nai-Pum for both of them were great favourites with their fellow-pages.

Baron Frederiks, who was afterwards appointed Lord Chamberlain in succession to Count Hendrikoff, had a nephew at the Imperial Page School when my husband was there. The Baron, an aristocratic-looking old man with his big hooked nose and large flowing moustache and heavily-lidded eyes, was very popular in Court circles.

Among the quaint court posts that still existed in the reign of the Emperor Nicholas the Second was that of the *Skorohod*. The literal interpretation of the duties attached to this particular Court dignitary was to precede important personages and to usher them into the presence of his Imperial master. For example, whenever a foreign Royalty or an Ambassador paid a state visit to the Russian Court it was the duty of the *Skorohod* to conduct them into the presence of the Tsar. Visitors of lesser importance were not honoured in this fashion, and it followed that anybody about the Court could judge the social status of an impending visitor at a glance. The literal meaning of the Russian title of *Skorohod* is rather amusing as well as appropriate to the nature of the work involved, for it means, " A person who walks quickly ! " Evidently the particular official who was in office at the time my husband was attached to the Imperial Court intrepreted his title literally, for Alexis has told me that he often barely had time to stand at the salute before the *Skorohod* and the important guest swept past him. This Court official used to wear a most elaborate uniform, while his hat was adorned with sweeping ostrich feathers that imparted quite a mediæval aspect to the wearer.

It was the custom at the Imperial Court for everybody to rest during the afternoon with the exception of the pages. They were left on duty in case their services were required, and used to take advantage of the general siesta to play and romp together like children.

The Imperial family led a very simple life except on State occasions. The Tsar was an early riser, and was fond of exercise. One of his principal hobbies was gardening, and he would put on an old blue-grey lounge suit and work away for hours

ROLL CALL OF THE IMPERIAL GUARD.
In the right hand corner is the Tsar's autographed signature.

Facing page 57

in his garden. He was also very fond of riding and driving, and during the winter months he used to go for sleigh rides in the Imperial Park at Tsarskoe Selo. On these occasions he would dispense with any guards, and go quite unprotected. It says much for his underlying bravery of spirit that he could do so in spite of the attempts made to assassinate him on various occasions.

The ladies-in-waiting at the Imperial Court did not receive any salary. Their names were submitted to the Empress by the Lord Chamberlain, Count Hendrikoff. But the final choice and selection rested with Her Imperial Majesty.

Reproduced on the opposite page is a specimen of the Roll Call of the Guard that has the Tsar's signature attached to it. The original document is one of my husband's greatest treasures, as there are few autographed signatures of the Tsar still in existence. It was certainly characteristic-looking with a dashing scroll underlining his name Nicholas.

The translation is as follows. At the top of the document is printed: " Roll Call of the Guard of the First Section, on the Main Entrance of the Winter Palace, during the presence of the Tsar." Underneath this is printed the following explanatory statement: " On this page are (A) Remarks of the persons inspecting the Guard. (B) Signature of persons who have been admitted to the Treasury Boxes which are placed in the Guards' Room. (C) Signatures of new and old Commanders of the Guard about the Changing."

Then comes the signed statement of the Grand Duke Constantine Constantovitch: " Inspected the Guard at five o'clock, six, seven, eleven, twelve and one o'clock at night from the 26th to the 27th of February, and found everything correct."

Signed : " Chief of the Military Schools."
" General Adjutant of the Tsar,"
" CONSTANTINE."

Below this comes the Tsar's own declaration :

" Inspected the Guard and Outside Posts at 10.30 a.m. on the 27th of February. Everything has been found in good order,"
" NICHOLAS."

In the left-hand corner two further signatures are appended :

" His Imperial Majesty's Pages' School."
" Captain of the Guard. KARPINSKY."
" Pavlovsky Guards Regiment."
" CAPTAIN GESCHTOFT."

The discipline at the Imperial Page School was very strict. Even reporting for leave of absence was conducted with quite ceremonial etiquette. In fact it was so lengthy that it sometimes occupied more than two hours. My husband has described it to me. It began by his marching up to the Camer Page on duty, and saluting him and saying : " Sir! X—— reporting for leave." At this the Camer Page subjected the applicant to a minute inspection, and if a button were not polished to please his fancy, ordered him to go back and repolish it. It frequently happened if the Camer Page were not feeling in the best of humours that the applicant was sent back no fewer than fourteen or fifteen times before the button eventually passed muster.

When my husband succeeded in passing the Camer Page on duty he had to report to the Superior Page Platoon-Commander. At such an hour the latter was generally to be found reclining on a couch and indulging in a brief rest. This might entail a further wait of half-an-hour or so, according to the mood of the individual commander concerned. During this interval the applicant was expected to stand stiffly at attention. When a commander intended to pass anybody at once he signalled his intention *by unfastening a button of his tunic*. When any applicant for leave of absence entered the room therefore, he used to give a surreptitious glance towards the commander's tunic in order to ascertain his fate.

Even when the Platoon-Commander had passed him the applicant's ordeal was not over, as he still had to pass the Sergeant. To reach the latter official meant walking down a wide room with beds ranged its full length. The sergeant's bed was placed at the extreme end, and as etiquette forbade any junior page passing round it, one was obliged to make a complicated detour. If the Sergeant made a gesture with his hand that was a signal applicants could proceed on leave. The last formality of all consisted of showing the pass to the officer on duty in the Guard Room.

There were occasions when the youthful pages succeeded in giving discipline the slip, and indulging in their natural high spirits and love of mischief. Once a small band of them decided that a young fellow-page did not wash himself enough, so they seized him and forcibly undressed him. Then, while several of them held his legs, and several attached themselves to his arms, the remainder poured the contents of a jug of cold water over his stomach. Naturally the victim did not enjoy this impromptu bath, and immediately he could free himself from his tormentors he retaliated by throwing a basin of soapy water over them. Unfortunately the majority of the water was spilt over the palace carpet, and splashed on the tapestried walls. This climax effectually damped their high spirits for the time being.

It was a strict rule that when the pages were on duty at the palace they must wear their knee-breeches absolutely skin-tight, and that not a single wrinkle or crease must mar the smoothness of the surface. The only way in which this rule could be complied with was for the wearer to thoroughly wet his breeches, and wear the damp garments next his skin without any intermediate covering between. But although this system was effective as far as preventing creases was concerned it necessitated the pages exercising the greatest care in their movements as, if one of them happened to make a sudden jerk, it might burst his breeches.

My husband once told me of an amusing " accident " of this sort that befell one of his fellow-pages. A State ceremony was in progress at the Winter Palace, and all the most prominent members of the Imperial family were present, among them being the Grand Duke Constantine Constantovitch. This prince had a deep-throated laugh in proportion to his immense height, and therefore, whenever he perceived a joke, everybody in his vicinity was made aware of the fact. As his sense of humour was apt to be rather misguided at times one never quite knew what was going to happen next.

At this particular function one of the Grand Duchesses ordered her page to adjust her train preparatory to making her curtsey to the Tsar and Tsarina. The page obediently knelt on one knee to do his Duchess's bidding, and as he did so his over-strained breeches split in twain with a noise like a pistol shot! The Grand Duke Constantine happened to be a close spectator of the incident. Unable to restrain his merriment at the sight, he burst into loud peals of laughter, and thus called everybody's attention to the luckless and crimson-cheeked page. I do not know what would have happened had it not been for the presence of mind displayed by one of the attendants who seized a cloak and flung it around the page's nether limbs. Thus, at any rate, decently draped, the embarrassed youth managed to sidle crab-fashion from the imperial presence.

CHAPTER 6

AT THE WEDDING OF THE EX-QUEEN OF GREECE

My husband's first State ceremony—Russian marriage customs —An Imperial betrothal—A youthful Grand Duchess and her reputation—The serious-minded Grand Duchess Anastasia—Rehearsals at the Imperial Page School—An Imp̦rial wedding in the palace at Tsarskoe Selo—Count Hendrikoff instructs the pages in their duties—When Court trains were twenty feet long—The Imperial procession— A magnificent spectacle—The Lord Chamberlain's Wand of Office—In the Imperial Banqueting Hall—A state dinner —A secret romance between two Royal lovers—The Grand Duke Michael Alexandrovitch as a wooer—At the Court Ball.

THE first State ceremony which my husband attended in his capacity as an Imperial Page was the wedding, in 1902, of the Grand Duchess Hélène Vladimirovna to Prince Nicholas of Greece, then the Duke of Sparta. It is curious that the title, Duke of Sparta, was only employed by foreigners in alluding to the Grecian Crown Prince, and that the Prince himself was unknown by it in his native country. The Grand Duchess Hélène was, as I have previously explained, the daughter of the Grand Duke Vladimir. She was just twenty and a very beautiful girl at the time of her wedding, and her marriage was regarded as an important event.

The Russian marriage ceremony is always a very impressive one, whether the bride is a Royal Princess or a commoner. A picturesque part of the ceremony is the holding of two golden crowns

THE EX-QUEEN OF GREECE 63

over the heads of the bride and bridegroom. This office is usually undertaken by the groomsmen who take it in turn to relieve one another when their arms begin to ache. There are numerous other quaint wedding customs. One is connected with a slipper. Instead of following the English fashion of throwing a shoe after a bride and bridegroom, it is filled with wine and passed round the bridegroom's friends for them to drink the health of the bride.

There was considerable astonishment expressed in St. Petersburg when the betrothal of the Grand Duchess Hélène to the Heir Apparent of Greece was announced, though I cannot say why it should have been so, unless it was because she had the reputation of liking all men and youths of her acquaintance to be in love with her so long as they took care not to let their love-making become too ardent. Probably this attitude of hers accounted for her pages being chosen for their handsome looks rather than their passionate disposition. To-day the Grand Duchess Hélène is an exiled Queen, and has been living in France since the fall of the Greek monarchy.

When her wedding took place in 1902, my husband was acting as page to the Grand Duchess Anastasia. She was the mother of the present Ex-Crown Princess of Germany, and a niece of the Tsar Alexander the Second. She is dead now. In those days she was known to be a very serious-minded woman. She held herself quite aloof from the frivolities of love-making that prevailed in the Russian Court.

Before the Imperial Pages were allowed to attend a Court function they had to be present at rehearsals in the school, and practise the correct method of holding up a Court train. Although these rehearsals were conducted with due solemnity they must have been amusing spectacles, as one of the pages would deputize for a Grand Duchess, and with a white sheet suspended from his shoulders and weighted at each corner to keep it down, would parade up and down the room, while the rest of the pages took it in turn to act as train bearers.

On the opposite page is a portrait of my husband wearing the uniform of an Imperial Page. Inset above it is a photograph of my father-in-law, General Alexander Nikolaevitch Ragosin. It was taken in 1878 after the Russo-Turkish War was ended, and shows him wearing the uniform of the Tsar's First Rifle Guards. I shall have more to say concerning him in a later chapter.

The uniform of the Imperial Pages consisted of white knee-breeches and black top-boots, and a black and gold coat ornamented with elaborate gold embroidery. Their gold and black helmets were rather like German helmets, as they had a golden eagle in front and a waving white plume attached to a golden spike.

It was arranged that the wedding ceremony of the Grand Duchess Hélène should be held at the Tsar's country palace at Tsarskoe Selo. *Selo* is the Russian word for village, but it is rather misleading in this case as Tsarskoe Selo was almost a country town.

The sixteen Imperial Pages were ordered to attend at the palace at nine o'clock on the morning of the wedding and to obtain their instructions from Count Hendrikoff, the Lord Chamberlain.

My Father-in-Law,
General Alexander Nikolaevitch Ragosin, taken at the close of the Russo-Turkish War, and showing him wearing the uniform of the Tsar's First Rifle Guard.

My Husband as a Youth,
in his uniform as Imperial Page to the Tsar, and wearing the medal presented to him by the Grand Duchess Anastasia.

Facing page 64

THE EX-QUEEN OF GREECE

The Count harangued them at some length concerning their general duties, and their behaviour at the coming wedding. He wound up by bidding them attend on their respective Grand Duchesses in order to take part in a full-dress rehearsal prior to the actual ceremony. Then he conducted the pages to the various Robing Chambers which the Royal ladies were occupying. Having announced his arrival by a discreet knock he held a whispered conversation with the inmates through the closed panels of the door, and then withdrew leaving the youthful pages inside.

The various rehearsals that followed took up a great deal of time as each Grand Duchess not only initiated her own page into the mysteries of her toilet, but insisted on his rehearsing the ceremony of carrying her train until every detail was perfect. My husband had to repeat his performance a number of times, and has since told me: " I shall never forget the length of the Grand Duchess Anastasia's train, or its weight when I first attempted to lift it. It measured quite twenty feet in length, and was made of white material ornamented by trails of artificial roses which hampered me still further by catching in the braid of my uniform."

The Imperial Pages were expected to manipulate trains gracefully regardless of their weight or their length. It was particularly difficult to do so when going round a corner, as etiquette demanded that the train should be kept perfectly straight.

While the rehearsals were proceeding, and the Grand Duchesses were finishing dressing, a procession of the members of the *Corps Diplomatique*, the Imperial Guards, and the prominent townspeople was formed within the palace. Marshalled into a long line these officials and dignitaries stood to await the coming of the Imperial procession.

This procession was headed by Count Hendrikoff, who looked a most resplendent figure. He carried in his hand his Wand of Office. This was a marvellous-looking cane with a knob entirely encrusted in diamonds and other precious stones. He advanced a few paces and rapped loudly on the polished floor with his wand as a signal to the watchers that the Tsar was about to approach. The soldiers stiffened to attention as the doors leading into the Tsar's private apartments swung slowly open, and the procession ushered forth headed by the Emperor and Empress. Two pages carried their gorgeous-looking trains. The Dowager Empress Marie Feodorvna walked behind her son and daughter-in-law, and behind her came a great company of Grand Dukes and Grand Duchesses, and their attendant pages. It is impossible to estimate the exact length of the procession, but it must have extended for several miles, in view of the fact that each Grand Duchess wore a train about twenty feet long.

Those present declare the spectacle was a magnificent one, with the women blazing in jewels, and the brilliant uniforms of the men making vivid patches of colour, while in the background were the curtseying rows of courtiers and townspeople, and the Imperial Guards standing stiffly at salute. The Imperial Pages withdrew when the procession entered the precincts of the private chapel, and were not present during the actual ceremony. When it was over the procession

THE EX-QUEEN OF GREECE 67

was re-formed and returned to the Tsar's private apartments.

The wedding ceremonies that day ended with a State dinner and ball. The dinner was held in the Imperial Banqueting Hall. This apartment had wonderful decorations, and on this particular occasion its beauty had been still further enhanced by masses of rare hothouse flowers, while the Minstrels Gallery had been completely concealed by exquisitely designed floral screens. Behind these screens sat the Imperial orchestra, which consisted of one hundred and fifty picked musicians. Their conductor was a Russian, named Varlih, and a brilliant musician.

All the guests sat at one huge table, designed in the shape of a Russian capital P. A court official stood behind the Tsar's chair, and at either side of him stood two stalwart-looking flunkeys. The uniform worn by this particular Court official was somewhat similar in its appearance to that worn by the Lord Chamberlain, with the exception of a golden key embroidered on the back of the tunic.

During the course of the dinner my husband was initiated into one of the little secret romances that abounded in the Russian Court. The two participators in it were the Princess Cecilia and the Grand Duke Michael Alexandrovitch, who was a brother of the reigning Tsar, and a son of the Dowager Empress Marie Feodorvna. In later years he married the Countess Brassow, but at the time of this wedding he was still a bachelor. Few things are hidden in Court circles, and so it was common knowledge that he was desperately in love with the Princess Cecilia, and that she returned his affection. Alexis was naturally interested in this particular Princess because he was page to her mother, the Grand Duchess Anastasia, and so he took special notice of everything she did.

Good fortune did not smile on this pair of Royal lovers, and even on this occasion they were separated by the width of the table. They contrived to overcome this check to direct communication by sending each other notes by their respective pages. This entailed the exercise of great precaution and diplomacy both on the part of the authors and the messengers, as neither wished to risk being caught by the sharp maternal eye of the Grand Duchess Anastasia.

Three years later the Princess Cecilia was obliged to bow to the dictates of Imperial policy and wed the Crown Prince of Germany. To-day she lives a retired life in Germany with her husband, and has only paid one visit to her autocratic father-in-law since his retirement to Doorn. This was on his much be-heralded birthday party.

To return to the wedding of the Grand Duchess Hélène and the Duke of Sparta: the Tsar and Tsarina retired to their private apartments when the State dinner was over, accompanied by certain favoured guests, and remained there awaiting the summons to the Court Ball. Their reaction to the strict etiquette and ceremonial that had prevailed until then was such that they relieved their feelings by playing games like a pack of children. Presently Count Hendrikoff entered, and informed them that everything was in readiness for the ball to begin, so once again the weary Tsar and Tsarina had to head a procession, this time to the ballroom. The Russian Court Balls opened with a quadrille, just as at the Court Balls in England, and after that dancing became general.

The Imperial Pages must have been very tired when the rejoicings connected with this wedding came to an end at last, for although a royal wedding may be a magnificent spectacle to the onlooker, it entails considerable fatigue on those who take any official part in it.

CHAPTER 7

MY CONFESSIONS

Should a woman have a lover ?—The greatest stimulant in the universe—A primitive emotion—How an Englishman woos—Lovers of various capitals—A language of the eyes and lips—My first proposal—An absolute Adonis—The Grand Duke André and a schoolgirl's foolish romance—Cave-man tactics !—Love letters by the hundred—A distorted view of an " Imperial Harem "—Wild rumours—I am given a Royal father—A romantic league—When I did the proposing—Compromising circumstances—Madame X—— threatens to shoot me—My husband opens my love letters.

WHEN I was a spinster I did not receive nearly so many proposals as I have since my marriage. I think the reason is that matrimony must have rendered me more attractive in the eyes of the opposite sex. It is generally acknowledged that a bud does not attain to its fullest and supremest beauty until it flowers.

On the opposite page is a photograph taken during my adolescent stage in my girlhood before romance really awakened me. Love is the greatest Gardener Alchemist on the face of the earth. This is not only because he is a stimulant but because—as far as a woman is concerned—he keeps her alive mentally and physically, and by acting as an antidote to staleness succeeds in reviving her beauty. Watch any woman who is really in love, and you will perceive a glory radiating from her that transforms her into a reflector of attraction.

I may claim to be a living example of my own

IN MY GIRLHOOD.

An early portrait of Madame Lydia Kyasht, as she appeared in a Ballet at the Imperial Opera House in St. Petersburg.

Facing page 70

MY CONFESSIONS

preaching for, not being in love, I look stale; and, what is infinitely more dangerous from an artistic point of view, feel stale. Such a statement is not intended to be regarded as a reflection on my husband, or my feelings concerning him, for I regard husbands generally as in a different category altogether.

Probably it will shock some people's sensibilities to learn that I believe it is a good thing for a woman to have a lover; but all the same, such is my inward conviction.

When I used to be on tour travelling about from one country to another I indulged in numerous flirtations with different men. Each affair gave me a deeper knowledge of life, and spurred me on likewise to achieve conquests in my art. Within limits they may be said to have formed the basis of the inspiration of my dancing. Personally I hold the opinion that if a woman is to succeed in one of the arts she needs a spur of this sort to help her to scale the heights, and that if she deprives herself of it she will never gain success. A woman who persists in making a bonfire of her emotions is also sacrificing her art, although she may not realize so at the time.

Our Russian men make love quite differently from English men. For one thing they are more emotional, and less self-restrained, but this is not surprising when one considers the dissimilarity of their mental and emotional atmospheres. For example, our men live at fever heat and extract every ounce from life which they can. A Russian man will kill himself, if need be, for the sake of the woman he loves. Should she, on the other hand, attempt to play him false he is quite equal to substituting her corpse for his own. Such a state of affairs may seem primitive to Southern eyes, but it must be borne in mind that the Northern races are more inclined to savagery.

Russian dancing epitomizes this spirit. It is wild and mad in its character and its construction. It is founded, like their wooing, on excitement. When a Russian man loves a girl, he puts forth the whole of his strength to the wooing of her. He courts her direct, and never attempts to approach her through the medium of a third party. Should she be married already, he will still pursue his love-making, and disregard a barrier that would be an impenetrable obstacle to a man of a different race and breeding. Now, Englishmen do not woo like this at all. I have known some who, when they were deeply in love, would suppress their emotions to such an extent that they ended by making themselves quite ill.

The fundamental difference between the English and the Russian man is that the latter regards the state of falling in love as a natural part of his daily existence, and would no more dream of suppressing his feelings than he would dream of holding his breath for an unlimited period. By comparison with the ardent-natured Russians I find the Englishmen are cold-blooded. They are the most difficult men in the world to vamp. I confess to having a weakness for a little vamping now and again, and that I find flirting is a diverting pastime, always providing that both parties regard it from the same standpoint, and that neither of them takes it seriously.

I think I can lay claim to having an international knowledge of men, as I have met some from most of the European capitals. I confess I hate Germans, and that I consider the best-looking men are the Viennese, while the Americans are the most direct in their love-making. This is judging from personal experience, for when I was touring the United States, quite a number of Americans fell in love with me, and promptly informed me of their feelings with a charming candour that was quite refreshing.

When a Russian man proposes, he does not say in so many set phrases, " Will you marry me ? " But he says it instead by inference, and employs a language of the eyes and the lips which every Russian woman comprehends.

I shall always remember my first proposal, if only because it was in the form of silent speech I have just described. My admirer was a fellow-countryman, and an engineer by profession. We met first of all at a party given by my great friend Tamara Karsavina. Her room was crowded with happy guests all laughing and talking merrily to each other. Suddenly the most handsome-looking youth I had ever seen in my life appeared in the doorway, and stood there scanning us all. It was Nicholas. Five minutes after my first glimpse of him, I had lost my heart to him completely.

He was a great favourite with women. They raved about him, and openly alluded to him as their Adonis. Anyway, he made me a charming fiancée, and we were very happy. Whether he would have been successful as a husband I cannot say, since fate decreed that we should not marry each other.

Romance always made an irresistible appeal to me even during my childhood. When I was about ten or eleven years old I became very enamoured of the Grand Duke André, a son of the Grand Duke Vladimir. André, who was cousin to the Tsar Nicholas the Second, was a remarkably handsome-looking youth of about seventeen. My childish mind was filled with all sorts of ridiculous dreams, and I used to wear his photograph next my heart underneath my prim schoolgirl's frock. It gave me a delicious thrill to feel it there, and I am afraid that even at that early stage of my career I liked to experience as many thrills as possible. André was destined to have a very romantic life, but I shall come to his love story in a later chapter.

I suppose it must have been at this period when my head was still filled with all kinds of romantic nonsense that I first conceived an admiration of caveman tactics. It was Karsavina who was really responsible for my initiation in this respect, for it was at her house that I met a little boy, Alexis. Curiously enough, this is my husband's Christian name. But the Alexis connected with this particular incident was another individual altogether. His father was the musical director at the Imperial Opera House. He was a very ugly boy, and the most noticeable thing about him was his propensity to display brute force on every possible occasion. He used to delight in knocking me about, and because cavemen were marvellous beings in my childish eyes I bore my bruises proudly.

One day Alexis presented me with his most treasured penknife. I took it back to school with me, and in an ecstasy of delight, proceeded to carve his name on all the desks in the classroom.

My offence was subsequently discovered by an indignant teacher, who confiscated the love offering. I was inconsolable at its loss until a fresh toy distracted my attention.

One thing I have refused to do is to make money out of any of my own romances. I recollect how an enterprising press agent once suggested to me that it would be good publicity if I would be photographed surrounded with bundles of love letters. He obligingly added the codicil that counterfeit bundles would do if I did not possess enough of the genuine article to make a lavish display. He was very disappointed when I refused to entertain his proposition, for I hold the opinion that love letters are intimate things, and not intended for public display. It has always been a practice of mine to burn any love letters sent me. Incidentally, had I commenced hoarding them I should have had to rent a safe deposit as a storage. There was one man alone who wrote me over five hundred ardent epistles.

When I first came to England I discovered that there was an idea prevalent everywhere that anybody connected officially with the Imperial Russian Ballet must have attained that position by being either a favourite of the Tsar or of one of the Grand Dukes. The general impression seemed to be that the Imperial Russian Ballet was a harem on a most magnificent and Imperialistic scale. It was nothing of the sort in reality. Probably, had it been so, we dancers would have led far easier and less strenuous lives, whereas as it was, we all had to work very hard for a living at salaries which would seem absolutely ludicrous to present-day stars.

Human nature being what it is, doubtless certain of the *ballerinas* found favour in the eyes of some particular Grand Duke. But how many stage favourites have not shared a similar fate? This state of affairs is by no means a sole monopoly of the Imperial Ballet.

All kinds of stories were set afloat about me when I first came over to England. One was to the effect that a certain well-known man about town had supplied me with a house in Regent's Park. But the wildest rumour was the one which gave me an Imperial father as a parent; no less a personage, indeed, than the late Emperor Alexander the Third!

Thus I found myself, through the vivid imagination of the local gossips, promoted to be a sister of a species of the Tsar Nicholas the Second. It was some consolation to me to think that the scandalmongers had at least given me a royal parent instead of a commoner, although why they elevated me in such a fashion I have never yet been able to discover.

These wild rumours that were circulated about me did not originate from my women friends for, although I frankly confess I prefer men to women, the latter have never been my enemies, but on the contrary have always shown themselves friendly towards me.

When I first met my future husband, Alexis, I was still engaged to Nicholas, the young engineer. Alexis was one of four brother officers in the Imperial Army who were ardent admirers of mine, and our subsequent love story I will describe later. Let it suffice to say that at the particular period I am describing it had not actively developed.

MY CONFESSIONS

These four officers formed themselves into the "Diana League," so named because that was their pet name for me. The sole object of the league was to marry me off to one of its members. One by one each of them asked me to be his wife, and each was refused until only Alexis was left. To my inward chagrin he did not immediately propose. The reason for this delay was because he was engaged to another girl, and was endeavouring to free himself. This he at length succeeded in doing.

By then I had decided that it was time to disband the "Diana League" so, with this object in view, I proposed myself to Alexis. But I confess that I made quite certain first of the answer being in the affirmative! Personally, I hold the opinion that if a woman really loves a man, it is infinitely better for her to propose herself to him than to wait; especially if he is at all inclined to be shy or tongue-tied. After all, if she feels shy about asking him straight out to marry her she can easily do so instead by a glance, or by a pressure of the hand.

In those gay days of the "Diana League" one little foresaw what tragedy the future held in store. Of the four young officers, my husband is to-day an exile with me, Alexander was killed during the revolution, Alexis Number Two married somebody else, and Basile Krevenko is an exile, like ourselves, and is living in Paris.

It was through the latter that I endured the most alarming experience of my whole life. This incident happened during the war. At that time Basile held a very high post in the Imperial Army. He was attached to the French Army, and was visiting St. Petersburg on official business. He occupied a suite at the principal hotel there. It so happened that I was also paying a brief visit to my country between my professional engagements.

My husband and I received an invitation to go to a large party which Mathilde Kschessinska, a former favourite of the Tsar Nicholas, was giving. We were staying outside St. Petersburg at Tsarskoe Selo, about thirty-five miles away, and as it was a long drive to attempt in evening dress my husband tried to engage a room at the hotel in which I could rest and change. But the town was crowded out and there was no vacant room. Just then Basile came to our rescue, and offered me the loan of his suite. I accepted the offer thankfully, and my husband arranged to call at the hotel for me and take me on to Kschessinska's house.

Now Basile had been having an affair with a certain married lady, a Madame X——, and was getting very tired of it. She had made the fatal mistake of taking the whole thing seriously, and he, in spite of his various affairs, remained very true to me at heart.

On the day of the party I dispatched some business in St. Petersburg, and went across to the hotel, where I proceeded to make myself at home in Basile's comfortable suite. I had brought a bag with me containing my dress and toilet requisites. Having enjoyed a bath, I slipped into a loose négligé in readiness for the hairdresser to come and wave my hair. After he had departed the chambermaid brought me some tea, and then I lay down and went to sleep.

Presently the sound of the telephone ringing awoke me. A woman's voice inquired for Basile, and on my saying that he was out, she demanded to be told who I was. Now although I did not actually know the identity of the speaker, I had heard about Basile's affair, and suspected it was Madame X—— asking for him. Foreseeing trouble, therefore, if I revealed my own identity, I answered that I was his sister. The effect of this speech was apparently still further to enrage the speaker, for uttering the one word " Sister ! " in a most sarcastic tone, she slammed down the receiver.

After this I went to sleep again, and was finally awakened by the entrance of Basile himself. He sat down on the end of the bed and we both smoked cigarettes, and discussed old times and mutual friends. In the middle of our conversation I recollected the mysterious telephone call, and told him what I had said. He declared it must have been Madame X——, and said she had threatened to commit suicide. I was advising him to have nothing further to do with such a woman when the door was flung open, and in walked Madame X—— herself. Doubtless to her distorted and distracted vision it looked a most compromising situation to see me lying on the bed draped in a flimsy négligé, and minus shoes and stockings, and with Basile seated at the foot.

She did not leave us in any doubt of her opinion concerning us. Walking straight across the room to us she addressed me, " I know you. You are Lydia Kyasht, and not his sister. You lied to me just now over the telephone. He is your lover."

With that she pulled a revolver from her muff, and pointed its muzzle dramatically at my breast.

I am no coward really, but the next thing I recollect is finding myself outside in the corridor. How I managed to get there I cannot say, but, at any rate, there I was and comparatively safe, although in a most embarrassing predicament, if anybody came along and found me there half clad. I was past considering convention. The principal fact of which I was conscious was that a heated altercation was being carried on between Basile and Madame X—— in the room behind me, and that the only barrier between myself and a revolver wielded by a woman, half crazy with jealousy, was a flimsily constructed door. Fortunately for me, my husband chose this moment to come along to fetch me for the party. He was astounded to discover me crouching on the floor, and shivering and sobbing with fright, so he promptly took matters in hand. It was a most unwelcome anti-climax for Madame X—— when he made his appearance in the bedroom. In the end he managed to pacify her, and persuaded her to let me off an early and unpleasant demise. But I sincerely hope that my only encounter with Madame X—— will be my last.

My husband has always trusted me implicitly. All the same when I came over to England he used to open my love letters and read them. I never raised any objection to his doing so, but I sometimes wondered what the authors of them would have said had they known, and also that the politely worded replies sent them, which bore my signature, were in reality written and signed by my husband.

He invariably used the same wording to this kind of letter.

"Dear A——,

"I am so sorry I am very much engaged at present. But perhaps a little later on you will call at the stage door, and my husband will meet you.

"Lydia Kyasht."

I have said that Englishmen make love differently to Russian men. To illustrate my meaning, let me add the explanatory footnote that not one of them pursued their suit for me even as far as the stage door!

CHAPTER 8

SIDELIGHTS ON RUSSIAN SOCIETY

The Tsarina's favourite Lady-in-Waiting—Russian parties and famous hosts—Favourite Russian dishes—When the Tsar gave a party—Those five entrances to Court Balls—Champagne with a golden ladle—Those souvenir-hunters—An over-greedy guest at an Imperial party—Lord Mayor of Petrograd—Madame Karsavina's handsome husband—An accomplished musician—Berednikoff—First public performance of the famous Swan dance—Patrons of the Imperial Ballet—Jet-black beard and ginger beard—Sentenced by the Checka—Popular languages spoken at Court—At a society party—The guest and his forgotten braces—A story of an eccentric Englishman—Easter festivities in Russia—The ceremony of the Tsar and the Easter Eggs—A freak Easter egg.

ENTERTAINING was done on a very magnificent scale in the Russia of pre-Bolshevist days, and some of the Princes and Grand Dukes used to give most wonderful parties. The Grand Duke Boris, who was a son of the Grand Duke Vladimir, and is a brother of the Ex-Queen of Greece, was a marvellous host. He entertained lavishly at his English villa, which was set in the midst of the Tsarskoe Selo Park, and was in its way a unique building. Of this particular villa and of Boris himself I shall give a fuller description later.

Madame Wyrubova was one of the most prominent society hostesses in St. Petersburg. This was chiefly owing to her undoubted influence with the Tsarina, whose favourite Lady-in-Waiting she was supposed to be. Although Wyrubova was very fond of the opposite sex she was never a favourite with the Grand Dukes, and they accepted her invitations more from a sense of duty than pleasure. All sorts of rumours were set afloat concerning her and her origin. The most absurd was that she was a daughter of the Grand Duke Vladimir, whereas her real father was Taneieff, an official at the Imperial Court.

She was imprisoned during the revolution, but she contrived to escape the death sentence that was meted out to so many of her friends, and is living somewhere abroad, I believe, at the present time. Probably the thing for which she will be most remembered is that she introduced the evil Rasputin into the Imperial household. Her husband was a naval officer, but the marriage did not turn out a success, and the couple were divorced.

Russian parties used to begin at a much later hour than is usually the case in other countries. Even bridge parties did not start until eleven o'clock, although the players made up for any delay in this respect by continuing their games until daybreak. A wonderful supper was invariably the climax to any Russian party. Hors-d'œuvre would be a feature of the menu, but not the meagre sort that is served in England. The Russian hors-d'œuvre consisted of about seventeen different kinds of dishes. *Vodka* was always served with it to give one an appetite. Otherwise champagne was the principal wine, but as I did not again experiment with it, its inclusion or exclusion made no difference to me.

Foreigners generally consider our Russian food is very rich. But we find it necessary to have it so in order to combat the severe cold of our climate. *Pirogeki* is a favourite dish. It looks like a long-shaped meat pie, and is served hot and eaten in the fingers like bread. Pastry figures a great deal too in the Russian menu. There is a delicious one, *Boubliki*, which melts in the mouth, while another popular one, which is served with the *Borsch*, or beetroot soup, is named *Vatrouschki*. This one resembles an open round jam tart with the exception that its centre, instead of being filled with jam, is filled with a mixture of sour milk and cream. Our principal fish is salmon or sturgeon. None of the cheaper varieties, such as haddock, brill, and cod, are much eaten in my country. Russians drink a great deal of tea, and the *samovar* is nearly always to be seen on the table during meals.

Whenever the Tsar gave a party all the food for it used to be prepared by the Imperial chef, instead of an order being given to an outside firm of caterers. Even the mere thought of doing such a thing would have horrified everybody.

My husband has told me about the wonderful Court Balls held in the Winter Palace, at St. Petersburg. The Throne Room was situated in the main hall, and the dancing took place in three other enormous halls. The guests entered by five separate entrances. One was reserved for the Diplomatic Corps, another for the Officers of the Guard, a third for ladies honoured with a summons to attend, and another for gentlemen similarly honoured, while the fifth and last was reserved for the citizens and townspeople. A buffet was arranged in each hall on which all the Imperial plate was displayed. Elaborately embossed gold vases were filled to the brim with champagne, and guests used to dip a golden ladle into the sparkling beverage and help themselves. All the company sat down together to supper. This was served later in the evening, and was like a banquet. It consisted of four or five courses of rich food and rare vintage.

Some of the townspeople had a bad habit of collecting souvenirs to take away with them. Serviettes were the chief favourites, and also chocolates and sweetmeats because these were always wrapped in silver paper with the Imperial crown stamped on it. If everything else in the way of a souvenir failed, guests would purloin one of the Imperial plates. But this practice was frowned on by the Court officials because the diminished china had to be afterwards supplemented at the expense of the Tsar's personal exchequer.

An amusing incident occurred once at one of the Court Balls in the Winter Palace. A particular Guards Officer was a guest. He was married and had several children, and had promised to take them back a souvenir from the Tsar's Ball. Etiquette compelled him to carry his helmet under his arm, so he made use of this custom to fill it to the brim with some of the choicest fruit and chocolates and sweetmeats from the Imperial table. He forget this temporary store-cupboard, and to the astonishment of the other departing guests and his own discomfiture, when he placed his helmet on his head preparatory to leaving, a rain of pears and nectarines and peaches and sweets descended on him. The story leaked out, and caused the greatest amusement throughout St. Petersburg. But the officer in question found it wiser to solace his "nerves" by a temporary absence from the Russian capital.

The Lord Mayor was an important public official in St. Petersburg. His official residence was the Duma, but he only used it as offices in which to transact business and never lived there, as the Lord Mayor of London lives at the Mansion House. We knew Glazounoff, the Lord Mayor, and his grandson Berednikoff. The latter was responsible for introducing Mochin—Karsavina's future husband—to her. Mochin was working in the Ministry of Finance. Her second husband is a Mr. Bruce. He was formerly attached to the British Embassy at St. Petersburg, and was reputed to be the handsomest man there. I was in the middle of practising a new dance the first time I saw him, and the sight of such a handsome man so distracted me that my lesson was ruined.

When Karsavina's son Nikita was born, a note was sent informing me that " Madame Karsavina has just had a son. Very big and tall. She is nursing him herself, but only for two weeks. After that she will have a nurse for him." Nikita has certainly fulfilled his early reputation for tallness. Although he is only twelve he is as tall as my husband. He is at Eton, and his mother adores him.

The Lord Mayor's grandson Berednikoff was an accomplished musician. He played both the 'cello and the piano. The first time that the now famous Swan dance was ever performed in public was when it was produced at the Dvorianskoe Sobranie, during a special matinée organized in aid of the soldiers who had been wounded in the Russo-Japanese War. I danced it and Berednikoff accompanied me on the 'cello. Afterwards Pavlova made the Swan dance famous in England and elsewhere. But I was the first dancer to create it.

Berednikoff was a great patron of the Imperial Ballet, and all the performers valued his good opinion. He and a friend used to share a box at the Opera House, and Karsavina and I were under their special protection. They were very good to us. They were a striking-looking couple; both of them were bearded. Berednikoff was very ugly and had a jet-black beard cut square like an Egyptian headdress, while his friend had a ginger one. When the revolution occurred, one of Berednikoff's most trusted servants betrayed him to the Bolshevists. He declared his master was an enemy of the people because he had a photograph of General Korniloff, the leader of the White Army. As it happened this particular photograph belonged to Berednikoff's parents. It had been in the family so many years that he had entirely forgotten its existence. It proved quite sufficient to give the Bolshevists an excuse to sentence him to death, and the Checka ordered him to be shot.

French and English were the two languages spoken at the Russian Court functions. As for the native tongue, one hardly heard it spoken on such occasions. Most Russians are good linguists and can converse fluently in several languages, and over there society women used to speak French and English as a matter of course.

The winter was the party season, and amusements went on continuously then from ten o'clock in the evening. Although my husband did not care for dancing when he was a youth, he was not averse to staying out all night with his fellow Guards officers until seven-thirty in the morning, and like the other officers was very fond of a game of poker. Card parties were always a very popular form of entertainment in Russia, and were as popular among the bourgeois or middle classes as in society circles. The citizens were great gamblers and not in the least like the middle classes of England or America. Families lived chiefly in flats instead of houses, and there was comparatively little home life.

An amusing incident occurred once at a large society ball. One of the Russian guests was a friend of my husband. He was noted for being terribly absent-minded, and on this particular evening arrived late just as an interlude occurred between the dances. Groups of guests were standing about chatting in the huge reception rooms as he passed through to greet his hostess. He was too absorbed in his own thoughts to notice their start of surprise and murmured exclamations as he went along. His hostess enlightened him for, as he bent his head to kiss her hand, she exclaimed in horror-stricken tones, " General X——, *look at your braces!* " The General had forgotten to conceal this necessary but homely portion of his attire, and they were hanging in festoons below his tunic.

There was another absent-minded guest, an Englishman, at a party. He was a very famous but eccentric man, and was so careless about his personal appearance that his hostesses never knew in what state of attire he would arrive. He surpassed himself at this particular party, for he arrived with a trouser button unfastened and his shirt hanging out! His hostess was too spellbound to say anything but, " Look at your toilet!" Her eccentric guest thanked her and proceeded to complete his toilet with perfect sang-froid in front of everybody. One wonders what the modern maiden, who if she ventures to powder her nose in public is criticized as a forward hussy, would have said to the conduct of this guest.

Easter was always kept up as a great festival in Russia. It quite superseded Christmas as an anniversary as far as they were concerned. The Court moved to the Kremlin Palace at Moscow for Easter, and went to the Crimea for the summer. Most of the well-known society people were the owners of large country estates, but went to stay at them to rest, and not for gaiety. In the country, therefore, the parties were mostly confined to picnics, and such simple amusements.

It was customary during the Easter celebrations for the Tsar to present an egg to a thousand of his troops in the Guards regiment, and to bestow three kisses on each soldier. Prior to this particular ceremony, therefore, a Regimental order was always issued forbidding the soldiers to pomade their moustaches. The Tsar himself used to have his own moustache specially prepared and perfumed for the occasion, and my husband has told me how soft and silky it felt. On the day, the three platoons chosen from the Guards regiments would line up, and when the Tsar arrived all the soldiers would shout together, "Christ is risen! Indeed, Christ is risen!" After this came the ceremony of the kissing, followed by the presentation of the Imperial eggs. The officers were also expected to duplicate this ceremony with the soldiers under their own command. My husband had to provide, on an average, a thousand eggs and brace himself, besides, to the ordeal of kissing a thousand men.

Freak Easter eggs were seldom used in Russia. I think one of the most amazing freak eggs I have ever heard about was one made by a certain chef of a famous West-End hotel in London. It had been ordered by a millionaire as a gift for his wife. The egg was a chocolate one. But its interior was divided into minute separate compartments, each of which contained a priceless jewel, while the centre of the egg was occupied by a chocolate cabinet whose small drawers pulled open and disclosed to view a valuable diamond in each. One imagines the lady in question must have been delighted at such a gift.

During the Carnival Week in Russia everybody danced, even when they were in the streets. Various character dances were performed also. But some people thought the rehearsals were the best part of the fun. The Guards officers had but little sleep themselves during Easter week, what with paying each other ceremonial visits, and continual feasting. When they arrived back at their quarters they were generally too hazy to have much recollection of what had occurred. Altogether Russian society in those pre-Bolshevist days, taking it on the whole, led a gay and carefree existence. Plenty of people since have said that society was dancing on its own grave. But such critics as these forget the mercurial temperament of the Russians. After all, as that renowned French statesman—the Duc de La Rochefoucauld —so aptly said in his classical *Maximes*, "The happiness and unhappiness of men depend no less on their temperament than on fortune."

CHAPTER 9

WITHIN THE PALACE OF THE TSAR

The betrothal of the Heir Apparent of Russia—A former favourite of the Tsar Nicholas the Second—Mathilde Kschessinska and her Imperial romance—Nicholas as Ruler —Marriage of the Tsar to Princess Alix of Hesse—A story of a trick played on the Secret Police—Coronation preparations—An uncle of the Tsar—The Emperor arrives at the Smolensk Station—On the way to the Uspenski Cathedral—The Imperial procession—A retinue of gilt coaches—The coach with the be-jewelled crown—My husband meets the Tsar in a relaxed moment!—The Duke of Connaught in Moscow—Marvellous Review—Another Royal visitor—Some of the Imperial palaces—In the Winter Palace at Petrograd—Its private theatre—A command performance—A certain rule—The Ermitage—An occasion when an Imperial Guard unbent.

NICHOLAS THE SECOND was twenty-six years of age when he succeeded on November 1st, 1894, on the death of his father, the Emperor Alexander the Third. He was still a bachelor, although his betrothal to Princess Alix of Hesse—a granddaughter of Queen Victoria—had been announced during his father's illness.

When Nicholas the Second was still Heir Apparent he had been very enamoured of Mathilde Kschessinska, the principal *ballerina* of the Imperial Ballet. But he discontinued his association with her after his accession to the Russian throne, and they only remained friends in a platonic sense.

Kschessinska had a most romantic career subsequently. She is now the wife of the Grand

Duke André, and she and her husband are residing in Paris. The alteration in her relationship with the Emperor did not affect her position in the Imperial Ballet, and she continued to play the leading part at all the special performances, and was known still to possess considerable influence and power in Imperial quarters. She possessed some wonderful jewellery which had been given her by her numerous admirers, and generally wore a massive diamond "dog collar," and ropes of diamonds and pearls which hung in glittering chains to below her knees.

Undoubtedly Nicholas the Second had a weak trait in his character that had not been apparent in his father, and which chiefly manifested itself in the way in which he permitted himself to be led by those for whom he had a personal affection. He was by no means the supreme autocrat that so many Emperors of the past had been. As for his continuing some of the suppressions instituted during his father's reign, he did so more from a wish to show respect to his Imperial parents' memory than because he himself shared such views. He introduced one innovation. This was to stop the persecution of the Jews. He accomplished this feat, moreover, very tactfully by dropping a hint in certain quarters that such treatment did not meet with his approval. Those who wished to be in favour in Imperial circles were quick to act on this hint.

Three weeks after the death of his father, Nicholas the Second married Princess Alix. It was said that King Edward, then Prince of Wales, advised his niece not to postpone her wedding on account of the Court mourning. The coronation

THE PALACE OF THE TSAR 93

of the Tsar and Tsarina was delayed for eighteen months after their marriage, and in the interim their first child, the Grand Duchess Olga, was born.

My husband was a pupil at the Alexander the Second Cadets School at the time of the coronation in May, 1896. Each cadet received a silver rouble, especially struck by the Mint to celebrate the auspicious event, as well as an enamel mug on which was engraved the Tsar's initials. Unfortunately Alexis lost both these articles during the revolution. A general feast was proclaimed in Moscow to celebrate the Tsar's coronation. The city was packed with visitors from far and near, and householders reaped a rich harvest by charging the most prohibitive rents for furnished houses for May and June, while one had to pay fifty pounds and upwards for a window from which to view the procession.

An announcement was made that presents of mugs with a picture of the Tsar printed on them would be given to some of the townspeople from certain districts. These could hardly be considered to be luck-bringers as indirectly they were responsible for the death of thousands. A Gala Fête was in progress at the Kodynshoie Polye (Plain), and the people were so eager to obtain the promised presents that they broke down the barricades which had been erected, and in the scenes which followed over two thousand men, women and children spectators were trampled to death. It was impossible to save the victims as, when the barricades collapsed, people were precipitated into the holes in the ground and subsequently crushed by the weight of the hundreds who fell on top of them. This catastrophe cast a general gloom over the rejoicings, and was regarded by many as a warning of ill omen for the Tsar.

During the coronation festivities Moscow itself swarmed with spies, and the Secret Police were kept busier than ever. The surveillance was so drastic that all sorts of people were ordered to leave the city, including a number of harmless students engaged in preparing for their examinations. Physicians also came under the ban of the Secret Police, and a number of them were ordered out of Moscow. This was a piece of folly for which everybody suffered later on, as when the accident occurred at the Gala Fête, doctors were much in demand, and there were not sufficient to cope with the situation and attend to the wounded persons.

There is an amusing story about a trick which a student successfully played on the police spies. This student used to read rather *risqué* French novels, and had packages of them forwarded from France. One day he received warning of the imminent visit of a police spy, and decided to prepare a little surprise in readiness. He tied up his novels into various parcels, and sealed the wrappers with the most official-looking seals he could find. Further to strengthen the illusion that these packages contained important documents he locked them away in a tin box and hid it in a cupboard. As he had anticipated, the spy instigated a thorough search, and on discovering the tin box, promptly confiscated it. What the Police said afterwards when it was opened, and its contents disclosed, was never revealed!

During the coronation festivities the entire railway line connected with the Yaroslav district

THE PALACE OF THE TSAR 95

was kept exclusively for the use of Imperial trains. The Grand Duke Serge Alexandrovitch, the Tsar's uncle, was then acting as Governor-General of Moscow, and £3500 was expended on upholstering his carriage. A wonderful pavilion was erected on the Smolensk Station for the reception of the Tsar. The central portion consisted of a drawing-room furnished in the French period, and most elaborately decorated. On arriving at the station the Emperor was met by six of the Grand Dukes, and conducted to the pavilion where a reception was held. After it was over he drove to the palace where a procession of priests greeted him. Each of them bore aloft a cross. The ancient ceremony of presenting the Tsar with bread and salt was then conducted with due solemnity by the priests, and the Tokens presented on a beautiful gold and silver platter.

The Tsar, mounted on a white horse, rode in his coronation procession through gaily-decorated streets thronged with people, to the Uspenski Cathedral. At twelve o'clock the cannons thundered forth a salute from the Tainitsky Tower, while on the Ivan Veliki the bells pealed a triumphant chime. As the procession approached the gateway of Moscow a salute of seventy-one guns was fired. The Imperial procession was a wonderful spectacle. Included in it were deputies from all over Russia. The representatives from Asiatic Russia were headed by the Kalmuck Chief-Mullah who, clad in a red dressing-gown, was a quaint-looking figure. Behind him walked representatives of the nobility and the Court, while the Imperial huntsmen, in their green and scarlet liveries, and led by the Master of the

Imperial Hunt, provided a picturesque-looking unit. The first gilt coach was drawn by six horses. Inside sat the two Coronation Masters of the Ceremonies with their Rods of Office. In the second coach sat the Grand Master of the Ceremonies carrying his Gold Stick of Office, surmounted by a priceless emerald. Behind his coach rode a procession of Kammer-Junkers in full dress uniforms lavishly embroidered in gold braid. Their three-cornered hats were trimmed with white ostrich feathers. A retinue of gilt coaches followed. And then came the Tsar. Behind him rode the Grand Dukes, and the Foreign Princes who represented the different nations. The Dowager Empress Marie Feodorvna sat in a gilt coach, drawn by eight white horses, each of which was led by a groom. A crown, studded with real jewels, was affixed to the roof of her coach. Last of all came the Tsarina seated in a gilt coach, the panels of which were decorated with mural paintings and eagles. It was also drawn by eight milk-white horses.

My husband had many opportunities of meeting with and talking to the Tsar, and thought him a very charming but very obstinate man, for all his vaunted soft-heartedness. Once when he was dining with the Guards officers, and enjoying a temporary relaxation from State duties, the Tsar remarked, "I feel like an escaped convict." Probably that was one of the few occasions in the life of that oppressed Ruler in which he felt utterly happy and at ease.

The Duke of Connaught represented Queen Victoria at the coronation and rode in the procession. Sir Alfred Welby, then Colonel-in-Chief of

THE PALACE OF THE TSAR

the Royal Scots Greys, was attached to the Prince's suite, and accompanied him to Russia. They remained altogether for three weeks in Moscow, and during that period attended innumerable banquets and receptions. On the Sunday a marvellous Review of thirty thousand troops was held on the ill-fated Kodynshoie Plain.

Another Royal visitor was the Prince of Bulgaria. Prior to this visit a schism had occurred between the Orthodox Greek Church and the Bulgarians, and the Orthodox Patriarchate of Constantinople had condemned them as heretics. Although the Russians had not openly expressed approval of this action, still the fact remained that they had acquiesced by their dumbness. Therefore it caused much satisfaction when Prince Ferdinand announced that his small son Boris was to be converted to the Orthodox Greek Church, and the former was at once invited to participate in the coronation ceremonies.

After the death of the Emperor Alexander the Third, his widow, the Dowager Empress Marie Feodorvna, inhabited the Anichkoff Palace in St. Petersburg. The Tsar and Tsarina occupied the Winter Palace there. This was a marvellous building, and had over three thousand rooms, and a private theatre capable of seating a large audience. It was about the same size as the Palace Theatre in London. I always looked forward to the occasions when I received a command to perform there. The stage was immense, and was stocked with every variety of scenery. It was a high building, and in shape was built to resemble a rotunda. The general scheme of decoration was carried out in white and gold and blue. This theatre was only intended for the use of the Tsar, and any Imperial guests honoured with an invitation ; so the seating accommodation was different from that of any ordinary theatre. There were no boxes or circle, and everybody sat instead in luxuriously upholstered fauteuils.

Whenever a foreign Prince was paying a State visit to the Russian capital, a command performance was usually given for him in the Tsar's private theatre. It used to be a dazzling spectacle to see the audience composed of ladies dressed in marvellous gowns and glittering with jewels, and Grand Dukes and Court officials in elaborate uniforms, and with their breasts ablaze with Orders.

Command performances were also held in the Imperial Opera House at St. Petersburg. As this theatre was the property of the Crown the Tsar attended performances there whenever he felt so inclined, and if any of the Guards officers were present they were instructed to stand stiffly at attention beside their seats for the whole of the interval. This particular rule was never relaxed no matter what the length of the interval.

Adjoining the Winter Palace was a large museum called the Ermitage, where a collection of pictures and statues were on view. The general public were admitted free of charge to this building.

Whenever the Tsar was in residence at the Winter Palace four of the Guards Regiments were on duty. These included the Cavalry, the Infantry and the Tsar's Own Body Guard. Within this palace was a picture gallery in which all the Guards colours were displayed. The private apartments of the Imperial family were situated

THE PALACE OF THE TSAR 99

in the centre of the Palace. The Throne Room, itself a magnificent chamber, was ornamented by marble columns, and a flight of marble steps led upwards to the throne, which was surmounted by Russian eagles. In every apartment the Guards stood on duty. They were immensely tall and looked most imposing men although they could unbend on occasion. Once an amusing incident occurred when Mr. Shearburn, the representative of Messrs. Maple of London, was visiting the Palace to discuss certain alterations in progress there. (It was Messrs. Maple who built the English villa for the Grand Duke Boris.) Mr. Shearburn had just had an audience with the Tsar about the redecorating of the Imperial nurseries. As he passed through the heavy doors, one of the Guards bent down and whispered in fluent English in his ear, " Excuse me, sir, but do you think your governor will win the Lincoln ? " This was the Russian Guards' interpretation of the status of King Edward, then Prince of Wales.

Like all newcomers, Mr. Shearburn was impressed with the Winter Palace and its wonderful decorations. He especially admired the elaborately decorated panels of the heavy doors. It is sad to think that to-day it is used as offices for the Bolshevists.

CHAPTER 10

ROMANTIC REVELATIONS

A self-made man—Monsieur Félix Faure—The French President meets the Emperor Nicholas the Second—The Tsar and Tsarina pay a State visit to Paris—The French President visits St. Petersburg and attends a command performance of the Imperial Ballet—Kschessinska plays the part of Venus—How I ruined the production and was nearly expelled from the Imperial Ballet School—An injustice to Russia—The true cause of Faure's unpopularity—His love affairs—His mistress—Why the French President committed suicide—A ridiculous tale—My dance partner—Serge Litavkin—His tragic love affair—A beautiful romance.

THE penalty of fame is that one's smallest actions become a matter for public comment, and this especially applies to anything in the nature of a love affair. Immediately a well-known man falls in love with a woman outside his own immediate circle, the world at large magnifies it into an affair. This was particularly noticeable in the case of the French President, Monsieur Félix Faure.

He was a self-made man, the son of a small cabinet-maker, and started in business himself as a tanner and merchant. He was a shrewd man and became very wealthy. When he was elected to the National Assembly he was only forty. After his election he interested himself chiefly in matters appertaining to the question of economics, and the improvement of the railways and the navy. He reaped the benefit of this policy thirteen years after, for in 1894 he was appointed Minister of Marines. Then, when Monsieur Casimir-Périer resigned the French Presidency the following January, Faure was elected in his stead. It was said that the principal reason for his unexpected elevation was because he was the only candidate for Presidential honours who offended nobody. Certainly he was a tactful man, and was always at his best on ceremonial occasions.

His first meeting with Nicholas the Second occurred when the Tsar and Tsarina paid a State visit to Paris in October, 1896. The French people regarded this visit as a most important event as it was the first time that a European sovereign had honoured their Republic with a State visit. The following August Faure himself paid a similar one to St. Petersburg. This was notable as being the first occasion on which the Tsar publicly mentioned the term " Alliance " in connection with France. As I have previously mentioned, his father Alexander the Third had already made overtures in that direction to France, but when the Tsar was on board the French man-o'-war he made a speech in which he formally used the expression " Alliance." This caused considerable satisfaction abroad.

The Tsar ordered a command performance of the Imperial Ballet to be held during the French President's visit. Our producer, Petipa, created an exquisite pastoral ballet for the occasion, and in order to give it the right atmosphere had two stages erected in the Imperial Park, and a huge artificial lake sunk between so that performers could be conveyed from one stage to the other by means of gilded boats. Naturally Kschessinska was playing the lead. She was taking the part of Venus. Karsavina and I were two of a bevy of Cupids selected to accompany Venus in the golden boat which had been specially prepared for the Goddess of Beauty.

Everybody was very excited, and Petipa was most anxious to impress the French President with the beauty and dramatic art of the Imperial Ballet. I was full of eagerness to second his efforts, and decided to introduce a little realism into the performance. In an evil hour I had collected a quantity of *Kliachka*. This is a sort of indiarubber that we used in the Art School, and I had discovered that if I inflated small portions of it, and clapped them against some hard substance, it produced quite a creditable sounding explosion. I decided therefore to do this at the command performance by way of introducing realism, and initiated my fellow Cupids into the entrancing sport. The result of our united efforts was that the otherwise impressive progress of Venus across the Imperial lake was marred at intervals by the sound of minor explosions! This unrehearsed effect was not at all appreciated by the powers that be. Kschessinska was frankly furious, and made her anger felt in such high quarters that Karsavina and I were both threatened with expulsion from the Imperial Ballet School. In all probability the threat would have been put into execution had not Petipa our producer intervened on our behalf, and obtained a remission of the sentence.

It was an unfortunate coincidence for me that my most mischievous pranks always occurred during State performances. It was still remem-

Two Famous Dancers, Madame Lydia Kyasht and Kschessinska.

Taken in France after Kschessinska's marriage to the Grand Duke André had taken place. (Madame Lydia Kyasht is seated on the right.)

ROMANTIC REVELATIONS 103

bered against me that I was the author of the grasshopper episode, and this time I had perpetuated a far worse crime. Kschessinska and I became excellent friends in later years in spite of this. On the opposite page is a photograph of us both taken in France after the revolution, and after she had married the Grand Duke André.

Some people blamed Russia for the French President's subsequent love affairs. They declared that Faure's association with European sovereigns had turned his head and made him cultivate habits generally considered the monopoly of Emperors and a frivolous Court. The latter speech was intended as a snub to the Russian Court with its underlying intrigues. Personally, I think such a criticism was not at all fair to Russia, and that a great deal of Faure's subsequent unpopularity with his own country people could be traced to the Dreyfus affair.

The year before his election as French President Captain Alfred Dreyfus, a Jewish officer of Artillery, had been arrested on a charge of supplying a government of the Triple Alliance with French military secrets. He had been tried by court-martial and sentenced to military degradation and life detention in a fortress. His trial was conducted in utmost secrecy in a manner resembling *Tcheka* methods more than anything else. But in France at that time all accused persons were presumed guilty until proved otherwise. English people find it hard to comprehend such an attitude as they pursue the opposite policy of believing everyone innocent until they have been proved guilty.

Félix Faure was very much censured for his

indecisive attitude concerning Captain Dreyfus, as although it was proved that the documents alleging the latter's guilt were forged and the author of them committed suicide, Captain Dreyfus, instead of being released, was sent again for trial, and sentenced to ten years' detention. While a heated discussion was raging over this and urgent representations were being made to Faure to grant a free pardon, the French President, instead of attending to the matter, was seeking consolation in the arms of his mistress. On February 17th, 1899, the newspapers announced that Monsieur Félix Faure had died the previous evening from an attack of apoplexy. But the most generally accepted story was one which stated he had been discovered in his mistress's bedroom and committed suicide to avoid the public disgrace. This particular tale found much more credence than the one which said he had taken an overdose of some powerful stimulant and then expired in Madame Steinheil's arms at her house. The sequel to this version was that Monsieur Clemenceau disguised himself as a doctor, and carrying in his hand a bag, visited the premises and secretly smuggled away the body of the French President. The only point on which all the gossips unanimously agreed was the one which declared Monsieur Clemenceau had a bag. This led a would-be wag to remark *à propos* of the "grand old man" of France that, "The 'Tiger' must evidently have mistaken himself for a 'stork'!" At all events Clemenceau was a staunch defender of Dreyfus. He was delighted when the former was exonerated in 1906, and made a Chevalier of the Legion of Honour.

Emile Loubet succeeded Félix Faure. He was altogether a different type of man, and not in the least addicted to illicit amours.

One of my dance partners, Serge Litavkin, came to a tragic end through a love affair. He was the son of a Russian general, and had partnered Adeline Genée at the Empire in London. He was never normal, and always weak and going from one extreme to the other. One instant he would be dwelling in the heights of bliss, and the next second down in the depths. Personally, I never applied the description "romantic" to his love affairs. They always struck me as crazy episodes more than anything else. It was generally believed there was a strain of insanity in his family, and this may have accounted for his peculiar behaviour.

Litavkin wrote a ballet called "Behind the Black Curtain." Curiously enough, in its conception and plot, it foreshadowed his own fate. When he was dancing in London he expressed a wish to live in the suburbs, so the musical director at the Empire, Mr. Cuthbert Clarke, gave him an introduction to a man at Golder's Green who owned a good deal of property, and Litavkin rented a house in that district in company with another Russian dancer, a much older man than himself. It must have been a curious household, for the triangle was completed by a little Russian dancer who was the mistress of the older man. Litavkin fell violently in love with her, and persuaded her to run away with him. They lived together for a fortnight, after which she left him, and returned —so rumour reported—to her previous protector. This blow proved too much for Litavkin, and he shot himself.

I was staying with a large house party in the north at the time of the tragedy, and Litavkin was booked to appear with me on the Monday at the Coliseum. Somebody sent a telegram to my host telling him what had happened, and asking him to break the news to me. The war was at its height then, and when I saw the orange envelope I instinctively guessed it contained ill tidings, and was afraid it referred to my husband, who was fighting with the Russians. Although I was grieved to hear of Litavkin's death, I could not repress a feeling of relief that it was nobody belonging to me.

Quite a different type of love affair was that of Madame Sokoloff. I have previously explained how she taught me dancing at the Imperial Ballet School. Her marriage with the naval officer was not a success, but the same complaint cannot be made of her subsequent love affair with Edward Goer. Their romance was the most beautiful one I have ever come across. They never married. Whether he was already married I cannot say, but he remained faithful to Madame Sokoloff until the day of his death, and devoted himself to making her happy. She had numerous other admirers but, as far as she was concerned, they had to rest content with a platonic friendship.

It was the custom for pupils of the Imperial Ballet School to pay a formal call on Madame Sokoloff every Sunday afternoon. She resided in a charming little house on the outskirts of St. Petersburg, and I always looked forward to going there on Sundays. She was by no means a young woman then, but possessed great charm notwithstanding. I can still see her sitting in her pretty drawing-room, the central figure in a row of admiring male visitors. The latter were chiefly elderly naval officers, and admirals with long grey beards and many decorations. They sat there gazing admiringly at their hostess, and kissing her hand at intervals. This was the utmost intimacy she ever permitted them.

During the revolution she and Edward Goer suffered terribly. He lost all his wealth, and eventually died from starvation. Two years after Madame Sokoloff also died. Tragedy follows so often on the heels of romance, and it was a tragedy that the beautiful dancer, who had delighted a Tsar and a nation, should fall a victim herself to the blind fury of the Bolshevists and die from starvation.

CHAPTER II

A SINISTER FIGURE

Hypnotic lover—My opinion of Rasputin—When I travelled in the same railway carriage with the notorious monk—His extraordinary physical strength—How he danced the Preesadka—A modern successor to Suslov—His sponsor at the Imperial Court—An indiscreet gift from an Empress—The Grand Duke Dmitry—A secret revealed—The future Tsar—An idol of the people—The Grand Duke's "unofficial" romance—Vera Koralle—The miracle-worker—Wyrubova is accused of faking an accident—When Rasputin performed a genuine miracle—The death of a tyrant—Sinister rumours—St. Petersburg hears that Rasputin has been killed—The Grand Duke Dmitry is banished to Siberia—Fury of the people.

SOME people have credited Rasputin with using hypnotic powers in his various love affairs. Judging from his personal appearance I should imagine that he must certainly have required the assistance of hypnotism to gain any prolonged success as a lover. He was the hairiest-looking man I have ever seen, and reminded me of a gigantic baboon. His enormous nose spread from one side of his cheek to the other, while his teeth were absolutely black, and could never have come in contact with a tooth-brush since they were first cut.

I remember once travelling in the same railway carriage with him. He sat on the opposite seat, with a newspaper held upside down in his hairy hand, and cast surreptitious glances at me from behind its shelter. I confess if my husband had

A SINISTER FIGURE

not been with me that feminine curiosity would have won the day, and compelled me to speak to the mysterious monk.

Rasputin had extraordinary physical strength. He would practise one particular Russian dance step, the *Preesadka*, for hours. This dance necessitates the performer crouching in a sitting posture, and shooting his feet rapidly backwards and forwards. It is very popular with English audiences. They have christened it the *Gobbler*, though for what reason I have never been able to ascertain. Rasputin used to dance it daily, and never displayed the slightest sign of fatigue.

It was said that Rasputin was really a follower of the *Khlysti* Sect, whose religious beliefs I have previously described, and that he regarded himself as Suslov's successor and the appointed representative of Christ for that particular generation. Some people went so far as to suggest Rasputin was a reincarnation of Suslov, citing as a reason for this belief the similarity between the two peasants in their abnormal powers of physical endurance. Certainly both were alike in bearing charmed lives in the face of a violent death. Judging from Rasputin's excesses it would seem as if he had combined two sects, the *Khlysti* and its offshoot the *Skoptsi*, and had adapted some practices from both to suit his own requirements. His father was a drunkard, so some of his worse vices may have been legacies from his parent. He was such a terror in his native village as a child that the old priest there paid him to stay away from church on the Sunday in order that the congregation should not be molested and disturbed.

It was Wyrubova, the Tsarina's favourite Lady-in-Waiting, who introduced Rasputin at the Imperial Court. He speedily attained great influence over the Tsarina, mainly because he was successful in curing the Tsarovitch of a severe illness after everybody else had failed. She was indiscreet enough to express her thankfulness in tangible form by making a shirt for him to wear. This action aroused much adverse comment in Court circles, although the Empress only intended it to be a slight expression of gratitude. The Tsar never liked Rasputin, while his cousin the Grand Duke Dmitry made no secret of the fact that he detested the monk, and thought his influence very harmful. Dmitry possessed great power over the Russian people, and was immensely popular with them. Many regarded him in the light of their future Tsar. But this belief was seldom openly expressed as the Tsarina's wrath would have descended on the holders of it. The Empress was passionately devoted to her son. She refused to look hard facts in the face and realize that the Tsarovitch's ill-health would probably prevent him from ever inheriting the Imperial throne. This delicacy of the Heir Apparent instinctively caused the people to look around them for a successor, and so, being attached to the Grand Duke Dmitry, they grew to regard him in this light. Possibly an exaggerated report about this reached the Tsarina's ears, and accounted for her jealousy of him, and her repeated attempts to discredit him in the eyes of the Tsar. Dmitry certainly failed to obtain the sympathy of the Empress, but he could always command the sympathy of the majority of women as he was a

A SINISTER FIGURE

very handsome man. In those days, in particular, women used to rave about his good looks. His father, the Grand Duke Paul Alexandrovitch, had incurred the displeasure of his nephew the Tsar by contracting a morganatic marriage with the divorced wife of a Russian, Eric Pistolkors. This gave the Tsarina an opportunity to still further widen the breach between her Imperial husband and his relations. Dmitry was credited with cherishing a romantic attachment for Vera Koralle, a dancer in the Imperial Ballet. She was also known in Russia as a film actress. Undoubtedly there was something between the pair, although would-be diplomatists endeavoured to cast the veil of "unofficialism" over the liaison. After the death of Rasputin several people declared that Vera Koralle had been present at his assassination.

Rasputin liked to pose as a miracle-worker, and many stories were circulated in St. Petersburg about the miracles he performed on the Tsarovitch. But one story expressed an opposite view. It asserted that the miracles were in reality fakes arranged by Wyrubova with the object of impressing her Imperial mistress. The most popular of these stated that she had had one of the palace chandeliers tampered with to give the monk an opportunity to rush in and to effect a dramatic rescue. This version did not prevent Rasputin from obtaining a substantial reward. The Tsar presented him with a magnificent jewel out of gratitude for his having saved the Tsarovitch's life.

Some of Rasputin's miracles were genuine enough, and I can vouch for one from personal knowledge. A friend of mine, a Mrs. Den, was the wife of a naval officer serving on board the Imperial yacht. They had a little son to whom they were both devotedly attached. One day this child was taken ill, and the doctors declared there was no hope of his recovery. Mrs. Den was a personal friend of the Tsarina, so when she heard the doctors' verdict she immediately telephoned the Empress and implored her to invoke Rasputin's aid to save the child's life.

" I will send him to you," promised the Tsarina. " Do not despair because, even if he arrives *after* your child is dead, he will restore the boy again to life." The Empress sent messengers post haste to fetch Rasputin, and the famous monk drove off in a fast motor car to Mrs. Den's house. On arrival he found the child was dying. My friend has often described the subsequent scene to me. Rasputin was taken straight to the nursery. He crossed to the cot, and laying his hands on the boy began to pray aloud. " It was a miracle when our child revived to life," she used to finish. This particular incident was the talk of St. Petersburg. Rasputin gained considerable honour and glory through it, and was further acclaimed as a miracle-worker.

At last the monk's excesses became such that some of the Grand Dukes held a consultation, and decided he must be killed. The two principal instigators were Prince Youssoupoff and the Grand Duke Dmitry. It was arranged that the former should persuade Rasputin to visit him at his house. What transpired there has already been described in detail. Suffice it to say that the monk appeared to possess a charmed life. It is commonly reputed to have taken a bottleful of

A SINISTER FIGURE

poisoned wine, as well as five shots from a pistol and a blow from a club, to kill him!

I shall never forget the night of his death. I had just arrived from England in December, 1916, to pay my native country a fleeting visit, and was shortly leaving again to fulfil my professional engagements. My husband and I went to a performance at the Imperial Opera House at St. Petersburg. It was the general custom there for everybody to congregate in the foyer during an interval, and we both went out to chat with some friends. That evening it seemed to me as if a curious undercurrent of excitement was permeating the atmosphere. I could feel the general sense of tension, and hear whispered fragments of conversation concerning Rasputin being bandied about from one person to another.

After the performance at the Opera House was over my husband and I went on to a party given by the son-in-law of the Minister of Finance. When we arrived there I was again cognisant of that sinister undercurrent. It was as if everybody was waiting in suspense for something to happen. Suddenly I perceived a messenger hastily making his way through the groups of guests towards our host. Shortly afterwards it was announced that Prince Youssoupoff had killed Rasputin, and that the Grand Duke Dmitry was banished to Siberia. People were furious on hearing Dmitry's fate, as he was a general favourite, whereas everybody in their heart felt relieved at the death of the tyrant Rasputin, even though his end was violent. He was a horrible man. Horrible in his personal appearance, and even more horrible in his ways. His name had been a menace to thousands throughout Russia. The idea therefore, that their popular idol, the Grand Duke Dmitry, should be banished to Siberia because he had helped to rid the Russian nation of a man who had been more beast than human being roused feelings of intense indignation, and the immediate release of the Grand Duke was demanded in no uncertain terms. Although the Tsar would have yielded and recalled his cousin, the Tsarina was adamant. She was too full of anger at the death of her revered Rasputin to listen to any extenuating circumstances put forward by the sympathizers of the Grand Duke.

CHAPTER 12

MY OWN ROMANCE

My first meeting with my future husband—Alexis is shocked at sight of the ballerinas and their ballet skirts—The Diana League—I am not allowed to accept a supper invitation—Identification by millinery—The comedy of a black and white hat—My brother consents to my accepting a supper invitation—That expensive semolina pudding—Circumventing chaperonage—Secret meetings—A wonderful supper menu—The climax of my romance—A sleigh ride to Viborg—My wedding day—Our wedding reception at the Imperial Yacht Club—Our brief honeymoon—The St. George's Cross for Valour—Telepathy—A curious coincidence.

WHEN my husband was a young officer in the Guards he differed in one respect from his fellow-officers. He was not the least interested in women. I can honestly say that, as far as he is concerned, there has been only one woman in his life—*myself*! Our first meeting was rather romantic. It occurred during a special performance of the Imperial Ballet, given every year in aid of a certain charity. It was customary for the Guards officers to come, and for some of the younger officers to help behind the scenes. General Ragosin purchased the tickets, and asked Alexis if he would care to go, and make up a party of friends to help behind the scenes, so, being disengaged, Alexis collected together a number of brother officers and they all came down. This was how the Diana League first sprang into being, and how I became so popular that, to use a well-known Russian expression, " Every dog knew me ! "

On this particular night Pavlova was dancing, as well as Karsavina and I, and a number of others, who have since become famous *ballerinas*. It was the first time Alexis had been behind the scenes of the Imperial Ballet, and he was shocked and embarrassed at the sight of us all clad in our tights and ballet skirts. Long afterwards I learnt that he and the other young Guards officers voted me the prettiest girl there, and decided to ask me out to supper.

They did so. I told them my brother George never allowed me to accept such invitations, on which they immediately suggested he should accompany me. I was obliged to explain he never went anywhere, but nothing daunted they asked if he had no wife or mother who could deputize. They were very disappointed when I replied in the negative. But I had no intention of invoking the aid of my sister-in-law. The members of the Diana League were not easily discouraged. They ascertained where I lived, and what clothes I wore in the street. This was clever of them, as it might have been difficult to recognize me in the distance without my ballet attire.

One day they were told I was shortly leaving for the theatre, and was wearing a black hat trimmed with white ostrich feathers. In the hope of waylaying me they set off in a *troika*, and drove to our house. But I had already started when they arrived, and they found themselves in a dilemma as black-and-white hats were very fashionable that season in St. Petersburg, and numbers of people besides me were wearing one. This resulted in an amusing comedy of errors, as whenever Alexis and his three friends caught sight in the distance of a black and white hat, they rushed off to intercept the wearer only to discover for their pains they had accosted a total stranger. How the comedy would have ended I cannot imagine but one of the four espied me driving past in a sleigh. Immediately they all rushed after me, and begged me to have supper with them. That day I was feeling extra high-spirited and eager for adventure, so I boldly summoned my courage and asked my brother's permission to accept their invitation. To my inward surprise he consented, merely making it a condition that I must be home early.

To the disgust of my hosts I insisted on choosing the simplest food at supper, and to this day my husband holds it against me that, for our first meal together, I ate semolina pudding. As a matter of fact, my simple little milk pudding cost them as much as the choicest viands on the menu because the restaurant at which we were supping was not in the habit of serving such plain fare, and so charged accordingly. Alexis declares my semolina pudding cost him and his friends nearly *three pounds*! But this fact I did not learn until much later. Then I was engaged to my young engineer Nicholas, and ought to have known better than to let my affections stray elsewhere. Alexis kept me company in this respect for he was also engaged. This was the reason he was so long in speaking to me about his feelings. Being a woman, I knew he was in love with me, although at first I pretended ignorance. The early part of any romance, where one can still tease and coquette, is one of the most enjoyable stages. Afterwards, when deeper feelings are stirred, one can only go with the current. It is useless to attempt to fight against it.

After that first meeting Alexis and his three friends became regular patrons of the ballet, and he himself attended every performance in which I was playing. We generally contrived to meet afterwards, but had to exercise great diplomacy because of my brother, and his rigid ideas on the correct chaperonage of unmarried girls. Needless to state, such views were diametrically opposed to mine, and we never agreed on the subject. Once I discovered George would be absent an hour and a half on business, so I told Alexis about this, and he and his three friends rushed round to fetch me in their *troika*. We all had a lovely time. When we returned, one of the four officers got out of the *troika* and went to see whether it was safe for me to venture indoors. He reported the coast was clear, so I ran into the house. When George returned he found me there looking very demure, and practising a new dancing step.

On another occasion I managed to evade George's vigilant eye and slip off to a supper party. It was being given in my honour and I was determined to go at all costs. My fiancé did not know I had accepted this invitation, and I was very careful not to enlighten him or my brother, because I knew they would disapprove and insist on my staying at home. The result was that when my hosts took me home they had to exercise great diplomacy to prevent George from seeing us together.

My hosts prepared a most elaborate feast. The hors-d'œuvre consisted of at least thirty different dishes, including caviare, mushrooms served in oil,

MY OWN ROMANCE

and meat balls mixed with cream and covered in a rich sauce, as well as all sorts of fish dishes. There were besides, my favourite small sausages grilled in butter, and *olivier mayonnaise*, which is a great Russian delicacy. We always have our vegetables richly cooked, and the potatoes were mixed with cream and melted butter and chopped olives. It gave them a very piquant flavour.

I confess that at this supper party I did not insist on eating semolina pudding. Possibly my continued association with the youthful Guardsmen may have accounted for my acquiring a more extravagant taste by this time. Matters continued like this for about two years and a half, and Alexis and his namesake, and Alexander and Basile each, in turn, acted host to me. Then, as I have explained, I began to lose patience and determined myself to propose to Alexis.

The climax came on the day that a large party of us, including Karsavina, drove off in sleighs to have supper at Viborg. It is situated over eighty miles from St. Petersburg, in Finland, and the sleighs only held two comfortably on a long journey, so I arranged to drive with Alexis. It was altogether a gay party. I cannot recollect the exact hour at which we all arrived at our respective homes, but I do remember Basile, or Alexander, saying that he must be back in barracks by seven-thirty, and if he was to do it we must all drive fast.

My husband's people held rather old-fashioned views. At first the idea of their son marrying a dancer from the Imperial Ballet shocked them, but afterwards they relented and consented to our marriage. My brother's consent had also to be obtained, and at first he was very displeased with me for breaking off my previous engagement.

I did not want a very large wedding, and so only a few near relations were invited to the actual ceremony. I remember a hunchback drove the cab in which I rode to church, and I regarded it as a good omen. My wedding dress was brown chiffon, and over it I wore a long fur coat. After the ceremony was over we went to a family dinner party, but later in the evening a big wedding reception and supper party was given us at the Imperial Yacht Club. There the revels were kept up until five o'clock in the morning. After that Alexis and I went off by ourselves for a drive, and that was the extent of our honeymoon as we both had to resume our respective duties the same day—he with his regiment, and I with the Imperial Ballet.

On the opposite page is a photograph of my husband taken during the Great War. He is wearing the Russian St. George's Cross. This is equivalent to the Victoria Cross, and is only awarded for great bravery. It was awarded him in August, 1914. So few had then received this decoration that he was only the ninth person to be so decorated. He was given it because when he was near the Austrian front he captured, under continuous heavy gun fire from the Germans, a heavy German battery and two platoons. Quite fifty per cent of his men lost their lives, and it was a miracle that he himself was saved. The bar to the St. George's Cross, which can also be seen in the photograph, was awarded him in 1916 for valour, together with the St. George's Golden Sword. He had kept the attack going for eight

A Photograph of my Husband, Colonel Alexis Ragosin, taken during the Great War, and showing him wearing the Decoration of the Russian St. George's Cross and Bar, awarded him for valour.

hours in spite of the fact that the right and left wings of his regiment were killed, and he fought on until the order to retire was given. It was said that his action saved hundreds of lives. But all this I had to learn from his friends. He will never speak of it.

There has always been considerable telepathy between my husband and myself, and this was once demonstrated in a curious fashion after our marriage. I was appearing professionally in England, and Alexis was serving with his Russian regiment. He was competing in a sailing race with other Guards officers. This race started about nine o'clock, and the competitors had to sail round a lighthouse. It began to blow and rain, and then my husband's boat capsized. It took him and those on board with him altogether from ten to eleven hours before they succeeded in passing the winning post, and coming in second. One of the competitors had the middle mast of his boat broken, while all the rest capsized or else suffered some accident. When Alexis returned home he found a telegram awaiting him from me asking if he was well. There was no possibility of my knowing what was actually happening, but I instinctively felt he was in danger. This is only one of many similar incidents we have experienced at various times.

CHAPTER 13

GRAND DUKES I HAVE KNOWN

How Russian Grand Dukes make love—The Grand Duke Michael Alexandrovitch and his unique reputation—His sporting qualities—His morganatic marriage with the Countess Brassow—The Grand Duke with the deep bass voice—The Grand Duke Boris and his pretty mistress—A marriage of convenience with a Montenegrin Princess—I dine with the Grand Duke Nicholas Nicholaevitch—His gorgeous palace—A delightful host—How a Grand Duke dwarfed me—The Grand Duke Dmitry as a serious patron of the Imperial Ballet—His American wife—A Grand Duke who was described as " hot stuff "—A Russian Prince who was nicknamed " Baby Boy "—My friendship with Prince Igor—Our last meeting—Romance of his brother the Grand Duke Gabriel—His fascinating mistress—Nina Nesterovska—My great friend and a brilliant conversationalist—The power of a plain woman and how she enslaved a Russian prince—A devoted lover—The comedy of the bull-dog who lived like a prince—Nina and I have an alarming experience.

It might appear to an outsider as if the Russian Grand Dukes spent most of their time in making love, and in being made love to, but one must take into consideration the fundamental fact that Russian men love differently from Englishmen, and that besides being more ardent, they regard love-making as an important part, if not the mainspring, of their life. As I have previously explained, if the object of their passion happens to be already married, they do not let that hinder them from making desperate love to her. Probably such a state of affairs is not ideal, or to be encouraged, but it existed in the Russia I am

GRAND DUKES I HAVE KNOWN 123

writing about, and it still exists in other countries, albeit not so openly. The difference in Russia was that if a man fell in love with a woman he would openly go and live with her. In any case, their liaison would be an open secret among their own circle of friends and acquaintances, and would be treated as a natural state of affairs. After all, if one is indulging in a liaison it is surely best to do so openly and frankly, than to hide it and behave as if one were doing a shameful action.

Among the Grand Dukes I knew personally, one possessed a unique reputation as far as love affairs were concerned, and that was the Tsar's brother, the Grand Duke Michael Alexandrovitch, whom I have previously mentioned was in love with the present Ex-Crown Princess of Germany. He had the reputation of being "*a very nice, pure man.*" I have heard this description applied to him by numerous people. My husband always thought him a great sportsman, and said he reminded him of the Prince of Wales in this respect. After the Tsar abdicated in his favour, he displayed his sporting qualities in quite a different light, for he refused himself to ascend the Russian throne unless the whole nation united in consenting to his accession. He went still further and begged the citizens to obey the government which the Duma had set up. The Grand Duke Michael Alexandrovitch disliked the ceremony and strict etiquette associated with court life, and as for politics, he hated them. He contracted a morganatic marriage with the daughter of a notary, the Countess Brassow, who had been twice previously divorced. This marriage did not find favour in the majority of the Russians' eyes because they considered it a further obstacle to his ascending the Imperial throne. This Grand Duke was killed by the Bolshevists in 1918, but his wife and eight-year-old son survived him, and came to England. George, the son, went afterwards to Harrow, and Countess Brassow is living, I believe, in Paris at the present time.

His Imperial uncle, the Grand Duke Vladimir, seemed quite an old man to my childish eyes when I was at the Imperial Ballet School, although as age goes to-day he was nothing of the sort. I was very fond of him, and delighted therefore to find him a member of the audience when I appeared in the Tsar's private theatre at Tsarskoe Selo to give my first solo dance. After the performance the Grand Duke Vladimir came behind the scenes personally to offer me his congratulations. He had an exceptionally deep bass voice. If he spoke in a whisper the sound carried tremendously, and if he was pleased his whispered praise could be heard all over the building. Or if he were displeased the audience were similarly enlightened. Fortunately for everybody concerned he was a very even-tempered man, and generally praised instead of criticized.

I am very fond of his son Boris. He was a marvellous ballroom dancer, and I will describe his English villa further on. When he gave parties at his villa, the daughter of a well-known Russian general acted as hostess. They both lived together for some time, and I often wondered what his godmother, Queen Victoria, would have said to this romantic attachment because, although she was commonly supposed to be devoted to her godson, she was also generally credited as being a strictly moral woman. This particular love affair illustrates the powerful attraction which two opposites can hold for each other. Elisieff was very fair and dainty-looking. She reminded one of a piece of Dresden china, while Boris her lover was quite the reverse, as he was plump and broad in build and figure. They are married to each other now, and since the revolution they both reside in France.

In 1907 the Grand Duke Nicholas Nicholaevitch married Princess Anastasia, a daughter of King Nicholas the First of Montenegro. It was a marriage of convenience, and as far as his mistress was concerned, was a tragedy. The latter was a famous Russian actress, Potozka; I will describe their romance later on.

The first occasion on which I met the Grand Duke Nicholas was at a rehearsal of one of the ballets. He had come to watch it, and expressed a wish to know me so a mutual friend presented me to him. The Grand Duke invited me to dine that day at his house. Russian dinners commenced at five o'clock, so I knew I should have plenty of time to get back for the opening of the ballet. I told the Grand Duke I had already promised to dine with my fiancé. But he refused to take no for an answer and I was obliged to postpone my dinner with Alexis, and accept instead the Grand Duke's invitation.

All sorts of exaggerated stories had been circulated in St. Petersburg about the gorgeous furnishings of the Grand Duke Nicholas's palace. Naturally after this I was consumed with curiosity to see its interior, and discover whether any of these tales were true. My Imperial host showed me over the palace, and I found it was a storehouse of art treasures. I became so fascinated in looking at them all that I forgot the time, and was late in taking my call at the theatre. As for the Grand Duke Nicholas, I found him a delightful and entertaining host. He insisted on my eating plenty of the delicious food he had provided, and declared ballet dancers worked so hard they needed sustaining with plenty of nourishment. He did not give me any wine to drink, and for that I liked him. Delicious soda drinks were prepared instead for me. The thing that most struck me about my host was his immense height, and in fun I complained that he entirely dwarfed me. He immediately retaliated by jumping on a chair, and demonstrating how he could transform himself into a giant if he so wished. Some people called him serious-minded, but I found him full of fun both then and when we met again on future occasions. He gave very smart parties once a month during the summer at his country estate.

I have already mentioned how popular was the Grand Duke Dmitry. He was the son of his father's first marriage. His mother was Princess Alexandra of Greece. Dmitry took the Russian ballet very seriously, and regarded it as a supreme art. Whenever a new ballet was produced his opinion was eagerly sought, and his verdict anxiously awaited. He was himself an expert ballroom dancer, and specially excelled at the tango. This was his favourite dance. Since then the revolution has changed everything for the Russians, and Princes—Dmitry among the number —have become scattered refugees on the face of the earth. I have been told King George was very

PRINCE IGOR.
A son of the Grand Duke Constantine Constantovitch.
He was assassinated by the Bolsheviks in 1918.

Facing page 127

good to him when he fled to England to seek protection from the Bolshevists. He is married now to a charming American girl, formerly a Miss Emmery, and I am certain he will prove a delightful and lover-like husband. After all, what more can a woman desire than a man who combines both the qualities of lover and husband?

I have heard his cousin, the Grand Duke André, alluded to as " hot stuff " ! Certainly this description was true of him in some respects. His cousin, Prince Igor, on the other hand, was nicknamed " Baby-Boy," because of his excitable disposition. Igor was the son of the Grand Duke Constantine Constantovitch, and we saw quite a lot of him as he lived in a wonderful palace close to my childhood home. He was the most irresponsible man I have ever known. I should say his best quality was his intense devotion to dumb animals. Horses were his favourites, and his *troika* was generally acknowledged to be the best equipped in St.Petersburg. Shown on the opposite page is a photograph of Igor. He was tall and broad-shouldered like most of the Grand Dukes, and had finely marked eyebrows and full cut lips. I admired his hands because they were such a blending of masculinity and artistic ability. His palms were unusually long.

The last occasion on which I saw Igor was during the revolution. I was paying one of my brief Russian visits, and he came up to me and said, " Lydia ! I shall have to get you to persuade Lord Lonsdale to give me a post as his Stud Groom." At the time this speech was uttered I thought it was intended as a joke, but it transpired afterwards that Igor made it in all seriousness, and that he really was in need of a job, and felt his only chance of obtaining one was to put his love of animals to a practical use. My conscience has often pricked me since then to think that, instead of extending a helping hand, I should have left him to his appalling struggle; for the Bolshevists first stripped him of all his worldly possessions, and not content with that took his life also.

His brother, the Grand Duke Gabriel, escaped from Russia, and is now living in France. He is a great friend of both my husband and myself. The story of his romance is a very interesting one. It shows too how a plain woman can often attract and hold a man longer than a merely pretty woman. I have frequently observed this myself, and have come to the conclusion a plain woman owes her victory to the fact that she knows she cannot rely on good looks with which to hold a man, and so she is obliged to cultivate her brain. As a result she is usually a past-mistress at the art of fascination, and employs it to such good purpose that nobody thinks of her looks because they are too enthralled with her personality. The Grand Duke Gabriel was a frequenter of the Imperial Ballet, and it was one of the dancers there, Nina Nesterovska, who fell violently in love with him. She was a great friend of mine. She was not at all beautiful, but was the wittiest and most amusing conversationalist I have ever met. She could describe persons and places so vividly that anyone listening to her felt they were actually meeting them in the flesh. After listening for only a short period to her conversation one forgot that she was stout and plain because her interesting personality absorbed one.

GRAND DUKES I HAVE KNOWN

I recollect that when I first heard about the romance between Nina and the Grand Duke Gabriel I thought in my own mind it must have been an attraction of opposites ; for he was very thin whereas she, to put it politely, was very plump. He was devoted to her just the same, and installed her in a wonderful palace in St. Petersburg. They were the most hospitable couple, and kept open house for their friends. Guests favoured with an invitation to their parties could rest assured of getting the most delicious food and the rarest wines. We spent many delightful evenings there playing poker, which was one of our chief amusements in Russia. The Grand Duke proved a most generous lover, and indulged all Nina's whims. She appeared insatiable in her demands, especially when she found she had only to express a desire for anything to have her wish instantly gratified.

I shall never forget one day when I went to their house and found Nina awaiting me in a state of great excitement. She refused to give me any explanation but insisted on my accompanying her upstairs. When we arrived there she flung open a door and ushered me into a new and most perfectly appointed nursery. What was my astonishment, on going towards the beribboned cot that filled the place of honour in the centre of the floor, to find it occupied by a hideous black and white bulldog instead of the infant I had half anticipated. This animal turned out to be Nina's latest acquisition and pet, and she explained to me that the nursery had been specially designed for its occupation. When I suggested a kennel would have been more suitable, she called me "cruel-hearted"! The dog was really a most ferocious beast. It had an unpleasant habit of biting any guest to whom it took a dislike. But in spite of this, Nina persisted in regarding it with eyes blinded by love, and called it by the most ridiculous-sounding pet names. She kissed and fondled it in a manner more reminiscent of Titania and Bottom in the "Midsummer Night's Dream," than the twentieth century.

After the revolution, the Grand Duke Gabriel married Nina, and she is living with him in exile in France.

When we were at the Imperial Ballet together she was one of my greatest friends, and we once shared an adventure that might have resulted in dire consequences to us both. It occurred before her romance with the Grand Duke Gabriel. We had finished our studies at the Imperial Ballet School, and decided to make a short tour of some of the provincial Russian theatres. We were booked to appear at Baku, a seaport overlooking the Caspian. Its natives are a most repulsive-looking people, and are half Caucasian and half Tartar by birth, which possibly accounts for their savage appearance. The men grow their finger nails to the length of birds' claws and dye them with henna, while they colour their long beards to a bright blue. The combination of these different shades makes them present a very alarming spectacle to strangers. Nina and I were ignorant of the fact that Baku was then one of the centres of the white slave traffic. The consequence was that strangers, especially if they were girls, were looked on with avaricious eyes by the procurers of this hideous trade.

When we arrived at the town, one of the native men approached us and with much waving and gesticulating of his henna-dyed hands, besought us to permit him to carry our luggage, and direct us to an hotel. We had unwisely made no arrangements concerning lodgings. But then one does not usually do so on a theatrical tour, and as both of us felt very weary and tired we accepted the man's offer of assistance. We received our first shock when we arrived at the hovel which he had glorified into an hotel. And our second, when shortly afterwards we discovered that our self-appointed porter had decamped with our luggage. But as both of us were due at the theatre immediately we could not wait for further investigations, but had to rush off and prepare for the performance.

Later that same evening Nina happened to meet an old friend of hers at the theatre, the Governor-General of Baku. He and his wife invited her to return with them and spend the night at their house, so I went back alone to our hotel. I was too exhausted to feel nervous at the thought of being by myself, but a slight qualm assailed me when I discovered there was no key or bolt to my door. However I felt too tired to do anything but undress and tumble into bed. For a while I lay shivering under the bedclothes, and when I eventually succeeded in falling asleep my slumber was disturbed by the sound of horrible shrieks proceeding from the adjoining rooms. I felt thankful when daylight dawned, and I could get up and dress myself.

It was necessary to go through the bar in order to reach the front door, and as I made my way through it that morning, I found it occupied by groups of the hideous-looking native men. A filthy-looking brute, with a blue beard that reached to his knees, was sitting amid the foremost group. He beckoned me to join them, on which I took to my heels in a panic, and ran from the building, never stopping in my wild flight until I reached the shelter of the theatre.

The climax came when the Governor-General and his wife learnt that Nina and I had taken rooms at the *Hôtel L'Europe*.

"What! Do you mean to say that you have been staying at that brothel?" he exclaimed. "Why it has the worst reputation of any place in the town. It is the hot-bed for the white slave traffic!"

Nina and I were too terrified on learning this to know what to do, but he acted quickly enough and insisted on driving us both back to the hotel to fetch our luggage. The spectacle of us driving up in the official carriage, and under the protection of the Governor-General, created quite a commotion at the *Hôtel L'Europe*. The natives flew right and left as if they already felt the arm of the law upon them. More amazing still from our point of view, our stolen luggage was miraculously restored.

After this misadventure we took up our quarters at the best hotel in Baku. There was no accommodation available until the "persuasive" powers of the Governor-General induced the manager to give up his own room to us, and take a temporary abode himself in the bathroom.

I often wonder what my fate would have been if Nina had not accepted that invitation to sleep at the Governor-General's house and had returned with me to the hotel, because she was such a chatterbox that everybody would have known our room was occupied, whereas I crept about like a mouse for fear of attracting anybody's notice. All the same, it was not the sort of experience that one would wish to endure twice.

CHAPTER 14

AT THE VILLA OF THE GRAND DUKE BORIS

Queen Victoria is credited with having an English villa built for her godson, the Grand Duke Boris—The true facts of the case—Messrs. Maple, of London, are given the contract to build it—A hundred British workmen travel to Russia, in the charge of Mr. Shearburn—An Imperial monosyllable — Interest displayed by the Tsar and Tsarina in the building of the villa—Scepticism of the Imperial Engineers — How the villa was constructed—Setting up a record in speed—The difficulty of the Russian language—Confusing habits—Mr. Shearburn makes a conversational faux pas—At the Russian Admiralty—The Tsarina is impressed at last—How the Imperial Nurseries were redecorated—Mr. Shearburn is presented to " Nicky "—The Dowager Empress of Roumania as a young girl—How she shocked the British workmen—The Grand Duke Boris gives a dinner party—A useful article is found to be missing—When my husband and myself borrowed a hundred roubles from the Grand Duke Boris, and the sequel.

I AM very fond of the Grand Duke Boris, who was in my husband's regiment. He managed to escape from Russia during the revolution. Boris was born at St. Petersburg on the 12th of November 1877, and was very pro-English in all his ways and likings. His mother, the Grand Duchess Vladimir, encouraged this trait of his in every possible way, and it was really she who originated the idea of having an English villa built for him in the midst of the Tsarskoe Park, although his godmother, Queen Victoria, was commonly given the credit of conceiving it by the Russian people. A report was circulated that Queen Victoria had spent over

VILLA OF GRAND DUKE BORIS

a million roubles on its construction, and had given this sum from her personal exchequer as a gift to her godson. The true facts of the case were quite otherwise. The Grand Duke Vladimir, at the instigation of his wife, commanded the London firm of Messrs. Maple to send over a representative to Russia to discuss the project of their designing a villa in an English style of architecture and building it for his son. Messrs. Maple sent over a Mr. Mason who returned with a contract for the work, and it was immediately put in hand. When preparations were sufficiently advanced the firm sent Mr. Shearburn to Russia to superintend the job. He is a fully qualified architect and has travelled all over the world, executing commissions on behalf of his own firm. His colleagues describe him as being a " master of men," and certainly he proved himself so in the way in which he carried out his difficult task of building this particular villa. A suite of rooms was provided for him in the palace, but he had to find and rent a house in which the hundred British workmen who were sent out with him could live.

I have previously mentioned the deep-sounding bass voice of the Grand Duke Vladimir. He could be very gruff and imperialistic sometimes, but in private he was always most approachable and kindly. When the plans of his son's villa were presented to him the drawings were still in a very rough and unfinished condition, and Mr. Shearburn felt very nervous as to what the verdict would be. But instead of showing any displeasure, the Grand Duke Vladimir looked at them and then uttered in his deep bass tones the one gratifying monosyllable, "*Approved!*"

The Tsar and Tsarina were both very interested in the building of their Imperial cousin's villa, although both of them at first expressed scepticism as to its ability to weather a Russian winter. The houses over there were built with walls of not less than three feet in thickness in order to withstand the intense cold, whereas the villa was being constructed on the British principle of hollow walls. The Tsar sent his Imperial engineers and architects to inspect it, and they all laughed at the absurdity of building such a type of house as that in Russia, and declared it could never withstand the inclemencies of their climate. In spite of these gloomy prognostications Mr. Shearburn went placidly on his way undeterred by either praise or blame, while the Grand Duchess Vladimir sympathized and commended in turn. She had had some personal experience of the merits and comforts of English buildings, as a portion of her husband's palace had been remodelled in the English style. She resolutely refused to be downcast at any of the depressing prophecies made by her friends.

The roof of the villa was made of English tiles. These were laid loosely in order that the immense weight of the winter fall of snow should not crack them. The upper part of the villa was of red brick and half-timbered. Red tiled gables increased its picturesque appearance. These were another innovation, as until then gables had never been used for Russian houses, and the tin or copper roofs had always been flat. All the ground surrounding the villa had to be cleared by hand. This entailed an immense amount of labour. The materials such as bricks, timber, and stonework required for its construction were brought on sleighs from Finland. The interior was designed to accommodate at least fourteen guests, and the necessary *entourage* of servants. Some of the bedrooms were decorated with hardwood fitments, and others with ash. Another innovation was introduced in the heating system. Hitherto it had been the custom to heat only *inside air*. But in this case the process was reversed, and the fresh air introduced instead into the corridors was heated by a special process.

The thing that most amused Boris and his brothers and the Russian architects was the speed at which the building was completed, as Mr. Shearburn only spent altogether twelve months in Russia, and during that period his workmen did extra work besides at some of the Imperial palaces. It seemed miraculous speed after the slow Russian method of house construction.

An amusing incident occurred during his visit which serves to illustrate the difficulty experienced by foreigners in speaking our language. I have often heard people say Russian is one of the hardest languages in the world to learn. The custom of naming a son after his father is a habit strangers find very confusing. For example, if the father is called George, the son becomes Georgaievitch, meaning literally that he is the son of George. Mr. Shearburn was provided with two interpreters, but I fancy neither of them fulfilled his duties as carefully as was intended; or else they could not resist the temptation of having a joke at his expense. At any rate one of them offered to teach him some Russian sentences, and Mr. Shearburn gratefully and unsuspectingly accepted. Shortly afterwards he was summoned to attend at the Yellow Drawing-room of the Palace to discuss certain alterations and redecorating with some of the Imperial family. While the discussion was proceeding Princess X—— came in. She is a particularly handsome woman and very gracious withal. Presently she asked Mr. Shearburn if he could speak Russian. Delighted at the opportunity of displaying a knowledge of her language he proudly replied, "*Your Imperial Highness, Ja vas loubliou!*" To his astonishment a dead silence followed his speech. Then everybody roared with laughter. Presently somebody explained to the puzzled Mr. Shearburn that he had told the pretty Princess he loved her. After this episode he eschewed Russian for the remainder of his visit.

Among the number of invitations which he received was one to a reception at the Russian Admiralty. There he shared the privilege with the French Ambassador of being the only two men present in evening dress. All the others were in uniform. It was a very striking scene to English eyes accustomed to more sombre shades. One lady present wore a deep orange-coloured dress, and had a blue Order slung across the front of her bodice, which made a vivid contrast.

When the villa was finally completed the Grand Duchess Vladimir was so delighted with it that she went to the Tsarina and informed her that, in spite of the predictions of the Imperial engineers, the house had proved to be cool in the summer and warm in the winter. Whether this plain speaking influenced the Tsarina or not I cannot say; but at any rate she immediately sent for Mr. Shearburn and instructed him to prepare designs to redecorate the Imperial nurseries in the English style. Until then the nursery walls had been hung with heavy silks and tapestries. On his advice these heavy materials were taken down and cretonnes substituted. The Tsarina was very curious to see what these cretonnes would be like, and gave instructions that they were to be brought to her immediately they were delivered from England. She was examining them in company with Mr. Shearburn one day when the Tsar suddenly entered the room. There had been so many conflicting reports circulated concerning the Emperor Nicholas the Second and his uncertain temperament, that Mr. Shearburn felt quite nervous at the thought of being presented to His Imperial Majesty. It was a distinct shock when the Tsarina called out, " Nicky dear, do come and look at these cretonnes! Aren't they sweet?"

Among other royal personages who came to watch the building of Boris's villa was the present Dowager Queen of Roumania. She was a young girl then, and used to astonish and scandalize the stolid British workmen by riding a bicycle about the grounds of the Imperial Park. Bicycling was not general in those days and this was considered a very bold and daring thing to do. As most people are aware, the Dowager Queen of Roumania is a grand-daughter of the Emperor Alexander the Second. Her mother was the Grand Duchess Marie of Russia, and married the Duke of Edinburgh.

Whenever I returned to Russia for a brief visit between my professional engagements in England and elsewhere, I always went to one of Boris's gay parties at his villa. The general public had bestowed the nickname of "*Incomparable Lydia*" upon me by then, and I remember his teasing me about it. On the opposite page is a photograph of me taken at that period, which shows me when I first appeared at the Empire Theatre in London.

In order that the villa should be as English in its interior as it was in its exterior, all the rooms were furnished in the English style. This led to rather an amusing incident at one dinner party at which I was present. All the guests had finished dinner and were beginning to smoke when their host discovered there were no ash-trays on the table. Boris called his Major-Domo and asked for some to be brought. The embarrassed man was obliged to confess that there was not a single ash-tray in the place. "I like England," said Boris in plaintive tones, "but why do they not give one ash-trays to use after dinner?"

With the exception of his Major-Domo, who wore the conventional English butler's garb, the rest of the servants were dressed in Cossack uniform. The cooking and food was absolutely Russian. Whenever we dined there very lengthy dinners of many courses were always served, and his chef made a speciality of the most delicious sweets. Boris also had a wonderful cellar, containing very choice liqueurs.

After dinner was over we generally played cards or baccarat. I remember one evening my husband and I had no money with us, and were obliged to borrow a hundred roubles from our host in order to play. Luck was with us, and between us we won over four thousand roubles including five hundred from Boris himself. This made him very cross as he disliked losing at cards.

THE INCOMPARABLE LYDIA!

Madame Lydia Kyasht at the height of her fame, as a
Première Ballerina.

CHAPTER 15

STORIES OF THE FIRST REVOLUTION

Leading up to the fatal 2nd of March, 1917—Riots and assassination—My husband is sent with four platoons to escort fifteen hundred mutinous Russian sailors to Siberia —Men like wild beasts—An incident when mob law prevailed—What happened to the victim—Cramped quarters —A nasty thrill — Arrival at Hingan Station—Mutiny of Third and Fourth Companies—Seven officers against seven hundred mutineers armed with knives—How the Commanding Officer quelled them—A red-hot revolution— At Ufa—Wholesale looting proceeds—A ruse to escape to Samara—Enforced stoppage at Abdonlino—The engine driver is arrested — A parley with the revolutionary leader —Universal strike proclaimed—Famine—A riot ensues —How my husband and his brother officers stopped it— A gruesome story—Strike-breakers.

THE events which culminated in the abdication of the Tsar Nicholas the Second on March 2nd, 1917, and in his subsequent arrest and assassination the following year really began twelve years previously, in the international disturbances following the termination of the war between Russia and Japan.

The year 1905 was ushered in badly for the Imperial family with the assassination on February 17th of the Grand Duke Serge Alexandrovitch, the Tsar's uncle. The following year began equally badly for them and for the whole nation, by the riots in Moscow in the course of which over a thousand persons were killed.

While the Russo-Japanese War was still in progress my husband was sent in company with four platoons from the Guards regiments under orders to convey fifteen hundred mutinous Russian sailors on active service to Siberia. As can be imagined, none of the officers relished their task. They were hopelessly outnumbered as the Guards averaged only about twenty as against three hundred and fifty of the mutineers. Before the officers left for Siberia they were informed by way of encouragement and a parting salutation that "The Russian sailors are like wild beasts. They will shoot you like dogs before you reach Moscow!"

My husband has told me of an incident that occurred during the journey. It certainly illustrates the ferocious character of these men better than any description could do. One day the officers heard the most appalling screams coming from the direction of the vans in which the mutineers were confined. They rushed off to see what was happening, and were confronted by a practical example of mob law, the victim of which was one of the sailors. His comrades had taken him captive and then stripped him naked, and were occupied in the pleasant pastime of holding his naked stomach against the burning bars of a red-hot stove. It transpired that they had caught him stealing some food, and so had summarily taken the administration of justice into their own hands. The wretched man was rescued by the officers, but not before his stomach was a mass of singed flesh. He had to be sent away to hospital and remained there for many weeks.

It took sixty-three days to convey the fifteen hundred sailors to Siberia. During a portion of that period the officers had to sleep in fourth-class

THE FIRST REVOLUTION 143

carriages where the only beds consisted of extremely narrow hard wooden benches. These cramped quarters had to serve them for sleeping and living in.

Their first unpleasant thrill awaited them at a small station called Hingan, which was situated near the Manchurian mountains. The incline was so steep that two engines were requisitioned to push their train from behind in order to prevent it from slipping backwards and precipitating them all to the bottom of the precipice.

When they arrived at last at Hingan they were greeted with the information that the Third and Fourth Companies had mutinied on account of lack of rations. Unfortunately there was a shortage of provisions. Owing to this the men had had their rations curtailed to one meal a day, and bitterly resented it. The difficulties of the situation were still further increased by the fact that the station, with the exception of two hanging lanterns, was in pitch darkness. These hardly served to disperse any of the surrounding gloom. However the Commanding Officer proved himself more than equal to the emergency. He was not the type of man to waste time in pacific measures, or in argument, being a believer instead in the principle of Action speaks! He proceeded to put this maxim to actual use. Gripping his revolver he strode forward to the mutinied companies, and addressed them as follows: " You blankety-blankety-darned-fools! How dare you! What do you blankety-blankety-sailors mean by it?" To further emphasize his argument he smashed in the face of the foremost insurgent with the butt end of his revolver. It was a case of seven officers against seven hundred infuriated mutineers, and he knew there was no time to lose if he was to acquire the whip hand. The sailors were desperate and were armed with knives, while the officers only had revolvers. Surprising to relate, the truculent attitude adopted by the Commanding Officer had its effect, and the mutineers subsided for the time being. The following day after things had calmed down the officers were instructed to explain to the sailors the reason they had been restricted to one meal a day, and how the shortage of provisions had necessitated such a precaution.

There were no unions at that time in Russia, and strikes had been hitherto unknown, although revolutions were unpleasantly common occurrences. When my husband was returning from taking the mutinous sailors to Siberia, he ran into a red-hot revolution which later developed into a general strike. At every stopping place along the line officers were greeted by precautionary rumours such as, " Beware ! There is a revolution ! You will get no further than Ufa."

When they eventually arrived at Ufa they found an appalling state of affairs already in existence. Looting was in full swing. Two chemists' shops had been razed to the ground, while the one piano shop Ufa possessed had been entirely wrecked and fragments of pianos were strewn all over the adjacent ground. There was nobody in authority to stop the looters in their wholesale wreckage because, with the exception of five policemen, all the rest of the Force were absent on active service in the Russo-Japanese War. The consequence was that the looters simply did as they pleased,

THE FIRST REVOLUTION

and took whatever articles or valuables they most fancied.

My husband and his brother officers decided that it was impossible to remain inactive at Ufa, so Alexis looked round and managed to get hold of an engine driver whose family lived in Samara, and who was anxious to get back to them. After some parleying he persuaded him to drive them all there. The next difficulty to overcome was how to get out of Ufa without attracting the unwelcome attention of the rioters. After some consideration they eventually hit upon the ruse of affixing a Red Cross to the front of their engine, and thus safely camouflaged managed to get successfully away. The driver went full steam ahead. All too soon further difficulties arose. Their engine was fed with petrol, and their stock was limited and speedily became exhausted. There was nothing for it but to stop and try and obtain a fresh supply of petrol. When they arrived therefore at a big station called Abdonlino the engine driver stopped, and all the officers descended from their coach, while he went off in search of petrol. He was promptly arrested by the revolutionaries. After this occurred my husband consulted with his brother officers as to the next best course to pursue. It was decided to interview the leader of the revolutionary party, and adopt with certain modifications the tactics of their own Commanding Officer. They did so and commenced the interview by saying : " There may be only fourteen of us, but each of us is heavily armed, and we shall not hesitate to shoot any of you on sight if the necessity arises. Our suggestion is that you parley with us instead of provoking us to take action." The leader saw the force of this argument, and arrangements were made that Alexis and his companions should remain at the station for the present until news was received as to the future course the revolutionaries were going to pursue, and whether any transport would be available to take them on their journey.

A few days later a universal strike was declared. The immediate result was chaos. More and more people poured into the station at Abdonlino, including train loads of emigrants from European Russia bound for Siberia. And at last the dread spectre of famine stared everybody in the face. One day matters reached a crisis. An appalling scene ensued as the rioters, driven wild with hunger, proceeded to wreck the station. My husband and his friends feared that a number of the people would be killed in the general panic, and in the hope of gaining the mob's momentary attention, they simultaneously discharged the contents of their pistols into the air. The sound of the shots had the effect of startling the rioters into a temporary quiescence, and Alexis seized the opportunity of the brief respite to hold a further parley with the leader. This ended in the disturbances subsiding for that day.

The strikers were quite as brutal in their methods of dealing out summary justice as the mutinous sailors had been. One day an engine driver refused to accede to their demands to drive them to some particular destination. They seized the unfortunate man, and burnt him alive in the stokehole of his own engine, before anybody could intervene to save him.

THE FIRST REVOLUTION 147

There were continual scenes of bloodshed and looting. The state of affairs was really a precursor of what was in store in the future for Russia. It was a harbinger of the period when our land was destined to run red from the blood of her hapless victims.

After my husband succeeded in getting away from Ufa, he was ordered to go to Moscow with his regiment for the purpose of quelling another strike which had broken out there. I think he and his brother officers must have possessed a talent for pacifying strikers, because they succeeded in quelling that particular strike within ten days of their arrival on the scene. At one time in America there was an official called a Strike-Breaker. His business was to break up any strikes the instant they occurred. I do not know whether such a post still exists over there now.

The whole history of Russia seems to have been written in the blood of her Emperor, and of her people. If one turns back the pages of history there is revealed a continual embittered struggle against the policy of suppression. Just as the younger generation battle against the ideas and restrictions imposed on them by a previous generation, so have the Russian people fought blindly on in a desperate effort to attain progress. That is really what lies at the foundation of all their discontent. They resent having their wings perpetually clipped by those in authority, in the same way that the younger generation resent having their actions controlled.

I like Mazzini's description of progress, when he writes, "*Progress exists, has existed, and will exist, because it is God's Law.*" In that single sentence he has compressed the whole meaning of the word. May it not be that Russia has been struggling to work out that eternal cycle of progress through the centuries of suffering which she has endured, and that her present suffering is the equivalent to the pangs of child labour that precede the creation of a new birth, and the ushering in of a new life ?

CHAPTER 16

FROM SEVEN POUNDS A MONTH TO FORTY POUNDS A WEEK

How I came to accept an engagement at the Empire in London—A great admirer arranges a private audition for me in St. Petersburg—A contract that caused a law suit—The Tsar is displeased with me—Effecting a compromise with the Imperial Ballet—My first arrival in London—At the Hotel Metropole—I am very miserable—An exceptional cabman and a strange coincidence—I run away to Bloomsbury—A three years' contract—My husband joins me in London—The producer at the Empire—Mr. Fred Farren—The ballet "Sylvia" is produced there—Story of the Ballet—Super-salaried Stars of to-day—A misunderstanding and a stormy scene—Treasured Press Notices—A lawsuit with my agent, Mr. Montague Leveaux—Sir Edward Marshall Hall is briefed as my counsel—His marvellous eloquence—The sequel to the case—What a friendly solicitor costs one—What the clairvoyant told me.

WHEN I was dancing in the Imperial Russian Ballet I was receiving the salary of seven pounds a month, while Pavlova was only getting twenty pounds a month. But then they considered the honour of belonging to the Imperial Ballet more than compensated for the meagre salaries paid to its Stars. I had heard of the princely salaries paid to *ballerinas* in England, and so when a great admirer of mine, a Mr. Oscar Stevens, informed me that a well-known agent was visiting St. Petersburg in search of a dancer to succeed Madame Adeline Genée in London at the Empire, and offered to arrange an audition for me at a private hall, I jumped at the opportunity.

The agent in question was Mr. Montague Leveaux, and the Directors of the Empire Theatre had commissioned him to find them a *Première Danseuse*. He was an astute man of business. Having seen me dance, he persuaded me to sign a contract, appointing him to act as my agent for ten years at a commission of fifteen per cent. This contract was the cause of a law suit between us seven years later. However, to return to the period, in 1907, when Mr. Leveaux first saw me dance at St. Petersburg. He immediately offered me a month's engagement at the Empire at a salary of forty pounds a week. Naturally I was elated at such a prospect, as forty pounds a week seemed a small fortune then in my inexperienced eyes.

It created quite a stir in St. Petersburg when I first announced my intention of leaving the Imperial Ballet, and accepting an engagement to appear at a London music hall. I was made to feel my action was almost in the nature of a crime. In order to comprehend such an attitude as this one must bear in mind that the Imperial Ballet belonged to the State and was regarded as a sacred institution by the Russian people. Pupils entered the Imperial Ballet School at the age of eight, and after being trained there for eight years were given a twenty years' engagement, and received a pension at the end of that period. The Tsar was extremely displeased with me when I first expressed a wish to retire. His principal cause of complaint was that the Empire was a music hall, and not an opera house, and in his Imperial estimation therefore quite outside the pale. At length a satisfactory compromise was arrived at by my agreeing to take a year's holiday from the Imperial Ballet, during which period I was to fulfil my engagements at the Empire. When the year had expired I was able to prove that I had kept strictly to the traditions of the Imperial Ballet, so the Tsar allowed me to resign.

However, I am anticipating the trend of events. I shall never forget my first arrival in London. My husband was obliged to remain behind in Russia on account of his military duties, so that I came over alone. Mr. Leveaux met me at Victoria, and took me to the Hotel Metropole where a room had been engaged for me. I felt utterly wretched and homesick. To add to my misery I could not speak one word of English. Feeling thoroughly unhappy I went straight to my room, and sat down and wept. Mr. Leveaux had told me to come round to the Empire after dinner, and watch the performance. But in my agitation I forgot the name of the theatre. I felt altogether too depressed and lonely, however, to contemplate the idea of remaining for the whole evening by myself at the hotel, so, taking my courage in both hands, and still crying bitterly, I went downstairs and contrived to convey by dumb signs to the porter that I wanted a cab. He fetched one. But when it arrived I did not know what address to tell the cabman to drive to. The knowledge of my helplessness made me burst into fresh sobs, and I stood beside the cab with the tears pouring down my cheeks and a sympathetic driver and hotel porter in attendance. At last I managed to utter the one English word I knew, "Theatre!" My cabman must have been altogether an exceptional man, for without more ado he drove me straight to the Empire.

Once arrived there I quickly dried my tears for Mr. Leveaux was awaiting me, and the sight of a theatre made me feel again on my native heath. For days afterwards I continued to weep, the only exception being the period when I was rehearsing. These were the only times when I felt in my element and at all happy. After a while I began to feel it was impossible to endure any longer the loneliness of being in a big hotel by myself, and so I moved to Bloomsbury. A less aristocratic quarter perhaps, but it had the merit of housing my dancing partner, and thus provided me with an opportunity to speak my own language, instead of being obliged to remain dumb or else converse in gestures.

I danced a Russian dance in my national costume for my first appearance at the Empire. It proved very successful. At the end of my month the directors offered me a further engagement for a year at an increased salary of seventy-five pounds a week. Subsequently I signed on for a second year at a hundred a week, and for a third year at one hundred and fifty. I refused to sign the first year's contract unless my husband agreed to it and accompanied me to England. In the end he managed to obtain eleven months' leave from his regiment, which is the period granted to Russian officers prior to their retiring from the army, and subsequently he joined me in England.

Our chief difficulty at first consisted in our ignorance of the language. In order to remedy this we arranged to take English lessons from a Russian tutor who was resident in England.

This was a mistake as both of us were so homesick for the sound of our own language that, instead of learning English, we wasted the majority of our lessons in talking Russian.

Mr. Fred Farren was the producer at the Empire while I was there. Although he could not speak Russian we did not experience great difficulty in making one another understand, as he was a master of mime, and we were able to converse by gesture. He promised to teach me English, and I promised to return the compliment by teaching him Russian. But I am afraid as a teacher I was not a great success, and that the extent of my tuition consisted in teaching him only two words, "*Dos vidania*," meaning "good evening."

Mr. Fred Farren and I appeared together afterwards in Leo Delibes' romantic ballet, "Sylvia." The musical director of the Empire, Mr. Cuthbert Clarke, arranged the musical setting for it. Mr. Fred Farren played the part of Pan, besides producing it. Miss Phyllis Bedells was Ianthe, and Miss Unity More, Eros, while I played Sylvia. The scene was set in Thessaly in a glade on the heights of Mount Olympus, the home of the gods. The story of the ballet is that Sylvia, annoyed that a mortal should have discovered the gods' retreat, draws her bow in anger, and shoots Amyntas in the breast. Then repenting of the deed she kneels beside him and tries to restore him to life. She is thus discovered by the mischievous god, Pan. The latter is delighted at the death of Amyntas, having regarded him as his rival for Sylvia's affections. In despair at her impotence to restore the shepherd to life, Sylvia implores Eros to do so. The climax of the ballet is reached when Pan pursues Sylvia and seizing her in his arms embraces her. In desperation she again invokes the aid of Eros. The latter descends from his pedestal and throws his protecting mantle round her, after which he drives Pan out of the glade.

On the opposite page is a picture of Mr. Fred Farren and myself as we appeared together in " Sylvia," and also a photograph of him in the character of the Dancing Master. He was a master of make-up, and I shall never forget his wonderful make-up in that particular part, or his long tight-fitting trousers, and the pair of remarkable-looking striped socks he wore. His wig was a triumph to the art of Willie Clarkson, and was the most realistic-looking shock of hair. It fell around his face in stray locks, and gave just the character touch that the impersonation required. Mr. Fred Farren made up his eyebrows that night in a style which has since been made famous by Mr. George Robey.

When I first came to England I thought the English stage a bitterly hard taskmistress because I was told to make two changes at every performance, and dance three numbers in the space of fifteen minutes. At the Imperial Ballet I had been accustomed to dancing only two numbers, and then resting for an hour. However the thought of the difference between the salary paid me there and the one paid me in England helped to console me for the extra labour entailed. Probably present-day Stars will consider forty pounds a week a miserably inadequate salary. But then salaries have increased since I made my first appearance at the Empire. I am not certain

WHEN BALLET WAS AT ITS HEIGHT.

Mr. Fred Farren in the character of the Dancing Master, as he appeared in the ballet of that name at the Empire Theatre, London.

(*Inset*) Madame Lydia Kyasht as Sylvia, and Mr. Fred Farren as Pan in the ballet "Sylvia," also produced at the Empire Theatre.

Facing page 154

that merit has always kept pace with the high sums paid nowadays to some of the Stars.

My ignorance of the English language sometimes caused misunderstandings during rehearsals. Once Mr. Fred Farren and I had quite a scene on the stage. He was producing a new ballet, and as a novelty had arranged an *ensemble* at the end in which he wished me to dance in turn with each member of the chorus. He conveyed his idea to me as usual by mime gestures. I was furious with him for wishing me to do such a thing, because none of the chorus were experienced *ballerinas,* and our steps did not fit in properly. So stamping my foot at Mr. Farren I refused to continue. A heated scene followed in the course of which I screamed at him in Russian and he retaliated in English. In the midst of it I caught the one word " rude." Now owing to my ignorance of the language I imagined rude was a terrible swear word. Feeling dreadfully insulted therefore at being sworn at in front of the whole company I promptly burst into tears. By this time Mr. Arthur Aldin, the manager of the Empire, had appeared on the scene accompanied by the Managing Director, Mr. Walter Dickson. Sobbing loudly I endeavoured to explain to both of them in a mixture of alternate Russian and French and broken English, how Mr. Farren had grossly insulted me. My husband added to the general uproar by joining in and storming at everybody in turn. In the end the storm subsided as rapidly as it had arisen. We were all as good friends, if not better. Animosity is not a failing of stage folks.

I used to save my press cuttings from the

English newspapers, although at first I could not read them. I remember being especially proud of a criticism that appeared in the *Observer* following my appearance in the part of Titania in "A Midsummer Night's Dream." It read: "Nothing more graceful and dainty has ever been put on the boards. Her graceful figure moves through the piece with beautiful simplicity and classical elegance." The *Referee* was also very kind to me on this same occasion and said that: "Kyasht was a beautiful and graceful exponent of Titania."

When I was playing Titania they billed me in the programme as "Lydia Kyasht, the *Première Danseuse Russe*." This was my favourite description. I wished my country to have all the credit of my dancing.

After my husband and I had been in England a while some mutual friends introduced us to a solicitor named Mr. Veasy. One day the question of Mr. Leveaux's commission came up in the course of conversation. Until then I had been regularly deducting fifteen per cent every week from my salary, and paying it over to him. Mr. Veasy offered to act for me without charging me in the matter, and advised my attempting to get this contract rescinded. He declared that any Court would say ten per cent was a sufficient amount to pay, and that when I had agreed to the higher figure I was totally ignorant of the usual rate of commission charged by agents in England. In pursuance of his advice therefore I stopped paying Mr. Leveaux the fifteen per cent. After a few weeks the latter threatened to take the matter into court if I did not pay up the balance that was owing. In the end he brought an action

SEVEN POUNDS TO FORTY POUNDS 157

against me and claimed five thousand pounds damages.

Neither my husband nor myself knew anything about the English law. We were so ignorant in fact as to the proper procedure that we only briefed Sir Edward Marshall Hall as my Counsel the day before the trial was actually set down for hearing. He was a marvellous advocate and fully alive to the value of playing on human emotions. He painted such a moving picture of me set down as a stranger in a strange country, and completely at anybody's mercy, and showed that I was so ignorant of my own commercial value as a dancer that any astute person could exploit me for their own benefit, that everybody's pity was roused on my behalf. His cross-examination of Mr. Leveaux was a masterpiece of eloquence and ability. When the latter left the box the atmosphere of the court was generally sympathetic towards me. Sir Edward Marshall Hall followed up his momentary advantage by asking the Judge to grant a short adjournment to give him an opportunity of consulting with his clients. Having obtained this he took my husband and me on one side and told us: " Now is your moment to effect a compromise with the plaintiff! " So Mr. Leveaux was awarded damages of five hundred pounds and I was freed from my ten years' contract. We paid Sir Edward Marshall Hall a hundred pounds for the brief, but it was well worth it.

There was a sequel to this case later when Mr. Veasy, the solicitor who had offered to act for me for nothing, suddenly demanded to be paid three hundred pounds for his costs.

It was a curious thing that prior to the hearing of Mr. Leveaux's action I paid two visits to a clairvoyant, whom I was in the habit of consulting, and who warned me I was about to quarrel with my agent, and told me on a second visit that I should lose my law suit. She was altogether an extraordinary woman, and once greatly disconcerted an American millionaire of our acquaintance. But that story belongs to another chapter.

I became very happy after I had settled down in England, and thoroughly enjoyed my work at the Empire; and I loved my audiences.

CHAPTER 17

THE GLORIES OF THE OLD EMPIRE THEATRE

When " ballerinas" were showered with diamond bracelets—How ballet received a new lease of life — Its death-blow—Directors at the Empire—" Dickie the Driver "—" Billy " Fitzwilliam—A well-known man about town—How Board Meetings were conducted then, and a bottle of champagne—Amateur theatricals at Peterborough—Our producer wrecks his hat—First night supper parties—A diplomatist—Mr. Arthur Aldin—When I was not in a flirtatious mood—Mr. Cuthbert Clarke, the musical director at the Empire—He pays me a compliment—The Stage Door-keeper—Two interesting personalities—Enter Revue—" A Day in Paris " and " All the Winners "—Pierre Vladimiroff—My dance partner—An unrehearsed effect, and how I danced my partner to order—A new stage—Mr. Farren collides with the footlights—Miss Phyllis Bedells follows suit, and I turn an unexpected somersault—An old stage custom—The Master of Claque—A Testimonial Matinée, and a galaxy of Stars—An amusing mistake.

I WAS the first Russian dancer to come to England as a *première ballerina*. Pavlova did not make her first public appearance there until two years after mine, in 1910. I remember introducing our producer, Mr. Fred Farren, to her after her arrival and telling him : " She will make a wonderful success in this country." My prediction certainly came true for she has been a great success everywhere.

With the exception of Madame Adeline Genée, England has had no dancer of conspicuous ability for many years. Over a century ago Maria Taglioni created a sensation in Vienna as a *première danseuse*, and afterwards took London by storm, and roused her audiences to such a frenzy of enthusiasm that when she took her curtain they flung diamond bracelets at her feet. It is doubtful whether the present post-war bank balances would permit members of the audience to throw paste bracelets, even supposing they were so generously inclined. Undoubtedly ballet was degenerating in England until the arrival of dancers from the Imperial Russian Ballet gave it a fresh lease of life. They restored it to its former eminence, and made the general public eager to see it again. After I joined the cast at the Empire, ballet reached the height of its fame, and formed the principal item of the programme. It was the revues which were first responsible for ousting ballet from its popularity, and the films may be said to have completed the disaster.

The other day I was looking through some old programmes, and came across one where the Bioscope was put down as one of the last items. That was only fifteen years ago. It is extraordinary to think that the Bioscope has achieved such a change of fortune in such a short interval that it has even supplanted the Empire, once regarded as the King of music halls.

When I went to the Empire the directors included Mr. Walter Dickson, Mr. Billy Fitzwilliam, and Mr. George Edwardes. Mr. Walter Dickson was a great friend of mine. He was very stout, with a red face. By profession he was a wholesale meat merchant. He took a great interest in sport, and was known by the nickname of " Dickie the Driver " because of his abilities as a whip, and the expert manner in which he handled his own coach and team. One of his most cherished possessions was a watch, which had been presented to him by Mr. Jim Selby—the famous professional whip—who was as much a household word to the members of the coaching fraternity as Mr. Lloyd George's name is to politicians.

After my arrival Mr. Dickson gave a dinner party for me at the Carlton. I sat between Mr. Arthur Aldin, the Manager of the Empire, and my old admirer, Mr. Oscar Stevens, who had been the prime instigator in getting me to England.

I remember that Mr. Dickson nearly collapsed from surprise on discovering I did not drink champagne. He was one of the hardest living men himself. He would stay up until three o'clock in the morning and then drive the coach down to Brighton, and be back in time for the evening performance at the Empire. It was not altogether surprising that he was only fifty-three when he died.

Mr. Fitzwilliam, one of the directors—whose full name was George Charles Wentworth Fitzwilliam, and whose father was a son of the fifth Earl Fitzwilliam—was commonly known to his intimates as Billy. He was a keen fox-hunter, and the master of the Fitzwilliam Hunt. He has a beautiful place near Peterborough. In the days of the Empire he was a well-known man about town. He was tall, fairly thick-set in build and clean shaven.

I do not think that in those days the Directors of the Empire were very hard worked. There was an amusing little story *à propos* of this. When Mr. Fitzwilliam arrived one morning to attend a Board Meeting Mr. Dickson greeted him with the tidings, "We shan't have a meeting to-day. There isn't enough business to transact." On receiving this piece of information Mr. Fitzwilliam's countenance fell lamentably, and he exclaimed, "Oh! We must have a Board Meeting, or we can't open a bottle of champagne."

He was an extremely popular host, and was very fond of amateur theatricals. On one occasion he asked Mr. Fred Farren to go down to Peterborough and produce "The Pantomime Rehearsal," and arranged for Mr. Farren to get leave of absence in order to do so. Among the amateurs taking part were Lady Violet Brassey, and Mr. Archie Weigall, who excelled at eccentric dancing. Before Mr. Farren went down he was warned by Mr. Fitzwilliam that he would not find it an easy task to get all the amateur cast together for rehearsals: "You see, you can never expect to get them before eleven in the morning, and not for long then because of luncheon. And in the afternoon they like to go off to visit some place of interest. And in the evening—well, they won't want to rehearse then. But still, do the best you can!" was Mr. Fitzwilliam's advice.

The result was that the unfortunate Mr. Farren nearly tore his hair out by the roots because of his difficulties in rehearsing his amateur cast. He said afterwards that he never succeeded in getting the whole of them together for a single rehearsal. In spite of this fact the play was a great success in the end. This is so often the case with amateur performances, where a special luck seems to follow the performers. Professionals, on the contrary, have to work hard and long in order to attain any of their successes.

WHEN VARIETY
REIGNED SUPREME!

The Empire Theatre at the height of its fame, and (*inset*) Mr. Arthur Aldin, its popular Manager.

Facing page 163

Mr. Fred Farren was not so patient when he was rehearsing the professionals, and sometimes waxed very excitable. Once when he was directing a rehearsal the Managing Director interfered. This infuriated Mr. Farren so much that he flung his hat on the floor and jumped on it, until he had reduced it to a shapeless mass. Having completed the wreck he rushed off to the Queen's Hotel, which was situated nearby, and which was a favourite rendezvous with the Empire crowd.

Mr. Walter Dickson used to give his supper parties at the Queen's Hotel after a first night. It must have been a great worry to the management because he always refused to give the order beforehand. His reason for delaying was because he suffered himself from a bad attack of stage fright on the eve of every fresh production, and always envisaged a failure. If the first night proved a success he would invite the cast to a big supper party at the Queen's. But if it was a failure everybody went supperless!

Mr. Dickson hated rows, and generally contrived to be out of the way whenever any trouble was brewing. My frequent storms must have been a distinct trial to him. The Manager, Mr. Arthur Aldin, was a most diplomatic man with a nice taste in cigars. He is very good-looking, as can be seen by glancing at his photograph on the opposite page. He looks like a military man, or a naval officer, and has very keen blue eyes.

Soon after my arrival he took me to lunch at the Savoy, and told me: "You will get all the men in London running after you." Not feeling in a flirtatious mood that day I replied primly, "I love my husband!" and chuckled inwardly at his crestfallen countenance. We were excellent friends for the whole of my engagement at the Empire, and still remain so.

I was very happy really at the Empire, and got on extremely well also with the Musical Director, Mr. Cuthbert Clarke. He paid me the compliment of saying I was very easy to please, and less domineering than Madame Adeline Genée. He had been there for over forty years, and as a boy used to live at Folkestone. He was very proud of the fact that he was the first person to step over the threshold of the Empire after Sir Augustus Harris had taken on the management, and had had the building reconstructed for variety purposes. Mr. Louis Hervé was responsible for introducing Mr. Cuthbert Clarke to the Empire. The latter saw Mr. Hervé's name billed, and promptly wrote asking him to be given a post in the orchestra. Mr. Hervé agreed to take him on. And that was the beginning of his long association with the famous music hall. After Sir Augustus Harris died, Mr. George Edwardes became the Chairman.

The Empire Stage Door-keeper was a Mr. A. J. Reynolds. In appearance he resembled a sergeant-major, and could be equally as firm in his tactics if the necessity arose. He has since adopted the profession of an estate agent, and has a very successful business in the Finchley Road. Two interesting characters at the Empire were the Ballet Mistress, Madame Katie Lanner, who was an absolute martinet, and the Wardrobe Mistress, Miss Hastings. The latter's post was certainly no sinecure. In those days all the dresses for the cast were made on the premises instead of being ordered from some fashionable dressmaker.

THE OLD EMPIRE THEATRE 165

The system had its advantages because it was possible to renew dresses and frocks at short notice.

When the Empire began to change the style of their programme and produce Revues, all the ballets were shortened. After Madame Adeline Genée left in 1908, a revue was produced called " A Day in Paris." Lieutenant-Colonel Newnham was the author of it. He was a journalist as well as a playwright, and contributed a number of articles to various newspapers. Before I went to America a revue called " All the Winners " was produced at the Empire. It was written by Mr. C. H. Bovill. Brighton figured prominently in the plot, and the opening scene was staged in the Hotel Monopole at Brighton, which everybody knew was just a thinly veiled pseudonym for the Hotel Metropole. Among the well-known stars appearing in it were Mr. Seymour Hicks, Mr. Barry Lupino, Mr. Fred Payne, Miss Maidie Hope, and Miss Unity More. My dance partner on this occasion was Perre Vladimiroff. Both of us appeared together in the Monte Carlo scene. This was an appropriate setting for him as he was a great gambler.

I remember an amusing incident in this respect which occurred when we danced together at Deauville. Vladimiroff and the Musical Director used to spend all their spare time gambling at the Casino. The latter became so absorbed that he used to rush through his business at the theatre as quickly as possible, in order to get back for another flutter at the tables, and conducted at such a speed that it barely gave us time to dance our steps. Vladimiroff became very annoyed about this. One evening when we had experienced greater difficulty than usual in keeping up with the conductor's *tempo*, Vladimiroff threatened to leave the stage in the middle of the dance. I was aware that Vladimiroff had lost a good deal of money himself in the Casino, and so as he went off in high dudgeon towards the wing, I danced several quick pirouettes after him, and alighting on my toes at his side whispered in his ear, " If you do not dance, you will get no salary, and then you will not be able to gamble ! "

Having uttered this dire threat I pirouetted back gaily to the centre of the stage, and continued the steps of my dance as if nothing untoward had happened. The audience remained blissfully ignorant that anything was wrong. My threat succeeded in subduing Vladimiroff, and we heard nothing further about his giving up his part. One of the first principles instilled into professionals is the importance of always keeping faith with the public, and to let an audience down on account of a personal grievance would be an unforgivable sin.

During my engagement at the Empire a new stage was constructed there. This led to a very humiliating incident for me. The new floor was made of teak. It is laid in sections like parquet, and is extremely slippery. On the first night we were using it Mr. Fred Farren started his solo dance, but he had only danced a few steps of it when he slid across the stage and came to an unexpected anchorage in the footlights. The audience took it to be part of the performance and roared with laughter. The bruised Mr. Farren picked himself up and warned the next performer, who happened to be Miss Phyllis Bedells, to be careful of her steps. Miss Bedells went on smilingly. But after a few steps she was likewise precipitated into the footlights.

After this Mr. Farren came up to my dressing-room and warned me that I might be the next victim. I thanked him and promised to take great care. There was a quick spin in the middle of my dance. When I attempted to do it on this occasion I turned a complete somersault, and sitting down with a thump in the middle of the stage burst into tears. Witnessed from the front of the house it must have been an amusing spectacle to see the principal *ballerina* sitting in a forlorn heap on the floor and sobbing bitterly. But I could not see anything amusing in it myself. The chorus rushed to my assistance and picked me up. I ran upstairs and hid in my dressing-room and refused to return, in spite of the fact that the audience were shouting for me. Mr. Farren did his best to console me, but all I could utter was, "Oh! the disgrace! The disgrace!" For days afterwards I felt bitterly humiliated.

The Claque was still in existence when I was at the Empire. This was a system which compelled artistes to pay out a weekly sum from their salaries to the Master of the Claque, in return for receiving applause and a nightly ovation from his followers. When an artist was earning about forty pounds a week he, or she, was expected to pay thirty shillings or two pounds a week to the Claque. I was let off myself with a guinea. If an artist took a firm stand and refused to pay, the Claque always revenged themselves by indulging in cat-calls or else by ruining the whole scene by applauding in the wrong place.

We had never had such a system as this at the Imperial Ballet, and I was quite bewildered when the Master of the Claque first visited me. He was a Frenchman named Masée, and was altogether a very queer-looking individual with his black hair and flowing beard. He invariably wore a shabby-looking black suit and greasy bowler hat.

Mr. Fred Farren always asserted that he never paid a penny to the Claque. Perhaps they thought his position as the producer exempted him, but I was not so lucky in escaping. The Master of the Claque informed me, with much wealth of gesture and eloquence, that he was prepared to ensure the " Incomparable Lydia an enthusiastic reception nightly at the moderate price of a guinea a week ! " Fortunately for artistes the Claque has died out as far as England is concerned since those days. It still exists in certain places on the Continent.

Mr. H. J. Hitchens was the manager of the Empire for twenty years, although latterly in name only as Mr. Aldin fulfilled all the managerial duties. After Mr. Hitchens' death in 1911 a Testimonial Matinée was organized in aid of his widow. It was held on Thursday, March 16th. It was a great success, and many famous artistes contributed to the programme. Miss Gabrielle Ray sang one of her popular successes called " Go Away, Little Girl ! " out of the musical comedy " Peggy." Miss Gertie Millar appeared with Mr. Joseph Coyne in a duet from " The Quaker Girl." There was an extract from a scene in " The Chocolate Soldier," while others taking part

THE OLD EMPIRE THEATRE 169

included Mr. George Graves, Miss Phyllis Dare, Mr. Harry Lauder, Miss Phyllis Bedells, Mr. George Mozart, Miss Unity More, and Mr. de Groot. I danced my famous Russian dance, and also a *Pas de Deux* with my partner, Von Zalesky.

An amusing incident occurred in connection with this particular matinée. My husband was uncertain what clothes to wear as everything had been so different in Russia. He approached Mr. Aldin and asked his advice therefore on the subject. "Oh! just put on a morning coat," said the latter briefly. But he had a terrible shock when Alexis turned up in full evening dress, which was the Russian definition of that particular garment. "For God's sake, either turn up your coat collar, man, or go and hide yourself!" exclaimed Mr. Aldin. I remember my husband chose the darkest corner he could find, and sat there feeling very sad and sorry for himself, and wishing the English language had never been invented.

CHAPTER 18

GLAMOUR OF THE FOOTLIGHTS

Advice to ballet dancers—My daily exercises—How Russians drill their bodies—French women have no sense of rhythm—English girls do possess temperament—An outlet for emotion—Is jazz dancing?—An unpleasant experience at Manchester—At Leeds—Not such jazz devotees—Serge Diaghileff's Season at the Alhambra—Leon Bakst writes "Narcisse," and I dance in it—Sir Frederic Cowen conducts his own comedy ballet—My performance at the Coliseum—My Corps du Ballet of English girls in "Faust"—The Philips Opera Company—My English home—Some amusing experiences in producing amateurs—A charity matinée at Daly's Theatre—"Colour"—My deputation of indignant society debutantes—Beauty is eventually sacrificed to art—Sir James Barrie burlesques Russian dancers.

To some people there is a certain glamour attached to the stage. But speaking from my own experience I think that any glamour there is consists in the satisfaction of achievement and not in any personal sense. My advice to all stage aspirants is to study until they become expert. If they wish to become dancers then they must learn everything about dancing, from the classical down to the modern ballroom dancing. And if they aim at success they must understand that that can be attained only through hard work. Beginners do not always realize the importance of exercising vigorously daily. They sometimes fall into the mistake of imagining that their performance every night at the theatre is sufficient exercise. This is utterly wrong. Whether I am fulfilling a professional engagement or not, I always practise for at least forty-five minutes every day. If I did not do so my limbs would become stiff, and my muscles would tauten. A dancer must never relax her care of her body for a single instant. If she does she will pay the penalty for her slackness by stiffened limbs and joints.

The English people do not really understand ballet. They imagine they do, but the truth is that they like to come to a theatre and see a dancer kick her legs. In the Imperial Ballet legs by themselves were only a secondary consideration. The principal aim was perfection of detail. We used to regard ballet dancing in Russia as one of the highest forms of art. We drilled our bodies to obey our slighest behest. But then our country was really the home of dancing. I do not think there is any comparison between Russian and French ballet work. The latter always seems to my eyes to be lacking in life. The French women do not possess a good sense of rhythm whereas the English women do. It is a curious thing that, although English people as a whole do not understand ballet, their girls make excellent ballet dancers. I have trained hundreds of English girls in my school, and I have never found that any of them lack temperament if given the opportunity to display it. In fact I have come to the conclusion that very few of them are as temperamentally cold as people declare, whatever their men folk may be in this respect.

With Russians dancing is an outlet for emotion. We have been accused of excitability. But our dancing is prompted in its essence by excitement. It follows therefore as a natural sequence that that emotion is the one most prominently portrayed. After all it is wiser to express one's feelings than to suppress them continually as so many people persist in doing. The Russian people had endured such a policy of suppression from thair autocratic rulers for so many generations past that it was in a natural reaction from such treatment that their national dances became wild and mad in conception. Our real ballet is best summed up as a kaleidoscope of rapid movement and colour, that fascinates the senses of the beholder.

Somebody asked me once whether I liked jazz. I do not dislike it, but neither do I regard it as dancing. It affords me no emotional outlet whatsoever. I cannot imagine it affording one for anybody who is at all artistic, although admittedly it might stir a person's physical senses.

Jazz was responsible for my having a most unpleasant experience once at Manchester in 1919. We were giving an afternoon and evening performance at the Midland Hall there, and had been looking forward to it, having been told Manchester people were such keen musicians and so artistic. However jazz had gripped them to such an extent that we danced to rows of empty chairs. One member of the audience sarcastically remarked afterwards, " If it had been an exhibition of decadent jazz, with negroid contortionists, or a ferocious Apache display, they would have been turning money away." I have never forgotten that experience.

When we appeared once at the Theatre Royal at Leeds, I thought we were going to suffer in a similar manner because only twenty-five seats were booked for our first performance on the

GLAMOUR OF THE FOOTLIGHTS 173

Monday evening. However, a speedy transformation occurred, and we were packed out for the remainder of the week. So Leeds could not have been so devoted to jazz.

That same year Serge Diaghileff produced a Season of Russian Ballet at the Alhambra. It ran for three months; which seemed a very short period to me after the ten months' run we had been accustomed to have at the Empire. I appeared in two pieces: in a phantasy of the period of Philip the Fourth which was called "The Gardens of Aranjuez," and a mythological poem by Leon Bakst, entitled "Narcisse," and for which he personally designed the costumes and scenery. In the original legend Narcissus is pursued by two nymphs who are in love with him, and whose lovemaking is interrupted by Echo. The Nymphs tell Narcissus that Echo can only repeat what others say. He deserts her in order to test this theory, whereupon Echo, who is in love with him herself, implores the gods to avenge her by condemning him perpetually to the pangs of unrequited love. The ironical gods promptly condemn him to fall in love with his own countenance reflected in a pool. Among dancers from the Imperial Ballet taking part in the season at the Alhambra were my friend, Karsavina, Lydia Lopokova, Leonide Massine, and a host of others.

Sir Frederick Cowen composed the music and also wrote the scenario of a very attractive comedy ballet called "Cupid's Conspiracy," in which I appeared at the Coliseum in 1918. It possessed a particularly fascinating valse theme, and during our performances there he personally conducted the orchestra. I suppose that the

Drop Act Curtain at this variety theatre must be famous all over the world. It is familiar to thousands of people. Mr. Byam Shaw designed it, and Mr. Joseph Harker, the well-known scenic artist, executed the painting. I was included in the group of famous artistes depicted upon the canvas, and so also were my two friends, Madame Adeline Genée and Pavlova.

When I produced the ballet in " Faust," I had a most successful *Corps du Ballet* composed entirely of English girls. The principal dancer was Miss Aline Philips, who had been a pupil of mine. Her father was connected with the Carl Rosa Opera Company, and when it went into voluntary liquidation he formed a company of his own, and called it " The Philips Opera Company." His wife held very decided views concerning the progress of opera in England. She considered that ballets had not been sufficiently developed in connection with opera. On the Continent of course the policy of combining the two together had always been pursued.

By this time I had quite settled down in England, and made a home for myself there. I was very fond indeed of my little house in St. John's Wood. The most precious possession in my drawing-room was my grand piano, and I spent many happy hours playing over my favourite Russian airs.

In a previous chapter I mentioned Mr. Fred Farren's experience with producing amateurs. I have had some amusing experiences myself in this respect. Once my friend, Miss Erica Beale, and I were arranging an All Dancers Matinée at Daly's Theatre in aid of a charity. One of the star turns was to be a Phantasy, in which I was dancing,

GLAMOUR OF THE FOOTLIGHTS 175

and a number of well-known society debutantes were taking part. Many of them have married since then, but the cast included Miss Nancy Bowes-Lyon (a cousin of the Duchess of York), the Marchioness of Queensberry (now Lady Dunn), Miss Estelle Bromley (Lady Makgill), Miss Sylvia Ogden (Mrs. Wills), the Hon. Ivy Stapleton, and Miss Barbara Cartland (Mrs. McCorquodale).

I asked Miss Beale to write a scenario for me, so she wrote a Phantasy entitled " Colour." I played the Spirit of Colour, and was supposed to be led colour-blind to the kingdom of the Queens of the Colour World, where I subsequently recovered the use of my sight. In order to give it an original angle all the Queens were portrayed as being debutantes of a hundred years hence. They had to have their faces and hair coloured to match the shades they represented. Thus the Blue Queen was required to have a blue face, and the Silver Queen a silver face, and so on. Each of them was attended by Maids of Honour and Pages, and the spectacle, when the whole were assembled together on the stage, was a very brilliant one.

When the day of the actual performance arrived the great question of make-up arose. Some of the debutantes indignantly refused to appear with coloured faces. A deputation of about six of them invaded my dressing-room, and assured me that if their skins were poisoned they should sue me for damages. Altogether there was a great to-do. In the end like most theatrical storms it blew over, and they agreed to sacrifice their looks temporarily to their art.

The subject of the dancer has formed a topic for endless novels as well as plays. When Sir

James Barrie wrote his clever burlesque, "The Truth about the Russian Dancers," he was so unkind as to portray one of us in the character of a guest at a house party, and unable to walk on the soles of her feet through having so constantly used the tips of her toes. One must not forget that dancing is an exacting task-mistress, and especially so towards ballet dancers. Walking is not good for us. Perhaps that is the reason that, after fifteen years' residence in London, I still did not know Regent Street from Piccadilly.

CHAPTER 19

MY AMERICAN EXPERIENCES

I sail for America to play in " The Whirl of the World "— " The Times " honours me with a leader—My arrival in New York—Pestered with Press representatives—An astonishing statement about me—My salary—Meetings with well-known American millionaires—Mr. George Butler— A great habitué of the Empire—Mr. S. A. Seligmann—My dresses—Difficulties with the Customs—Lopokova in Cabaret —The story of her six hairs—A notorious Star—Gaby Deslys—Her little dog—Meeting Mrs. Vernon Castle—An attack of typhoid fever stops my engagement at the Winter Garden Theatre, Broadway—A rich millionaire banker— What the clairvoyant said to him, and his subsequent embarrassment—My own opinion of clairvoyance.

In December, 1913, I concluded a five years' engagement at the Empire, and shortly afterwards sailed for New York to appear as the Blue Bird in " The Whirl of the World." This was staged at the Winter Garden Theatre, Broadway, which belonged to Mr. Shubert. Before I sailed, *The Times* paid me the great compliment of writing a leading article about me, and publishing it upon their leader page. I was immensely thrilled, and make no apology for quoting the whole of it here.

" *Times.* Saturday, December 20th, 1913.

" Last night Mademoiselle Kyasht concluded a five years' engagement at the Empire Theatre. It is upon record that in 1881 a critic declared in desperation that a dancer to match those of the beginning of the century could only be found by travelling as far as St. Petersburg. In 1908 his prophecy was curiously fulfilled, for the Directors of the Empire Theatre actually went to Russia, as they would have gone, we fancy, if necessary, to ' the farthest Steppe of India,' in order to find what seemed an impossibility, a worthy successor to Adeline Genée.

"Mademoiselle Lydia Kyasht was the first Russian *ballerina* to be seen in London. Her success is attested by the fact that London greedily asked for more. Had Mademoiselle Kyasht made less of a triumph, it is doubtful whether Pavlova and Karsavina would ever have crossed the Channel. Thus, in a sense, it was she who made comparisons possible, but she has never had anything to fear from comparisons. Indeed, to contrast Mademoiselle Kyasht with her predecessor, Genée, or her two Russian sister graces, is simply to give relief to her own characteristic excellences. *Between her and the others there is a wide difference of personality.*

" Their peculiar charm, whether it is the merriment whereby Genée persuades us that she dances for pleasure, if not for fun, or the impalpability which makes Pavlova's *giselle* the ideal embodiment of the romantic dream of the thirties, or the sadness of Karsavina's eyes, which seem to reflect the melancholy of Russia's plains, is in each case relatively independent of their dancing ; it is an additional aroma surrounding their art.

" With Mademoiselle Kyasht, on the other hand, personality is in a unique degree fused with technique. She displays an almost hieratic concentration of her task, and her task, as she conceives it, would seem to begin and end with achievement of physical grace. Mademoiselle Kyasht would never make an actress, but she is unsurpassable as a formal and decorative dancer.

"Hence were we asked to say in which of the parts she has played in London she was seen at her best, we should unhesitatingly choose, not her rather frigid rendering of Sylvia, an amorous nymph, but her masterly impersonation of Coppelia, the living automaton. We should come nearest of all to the truth perhaps if we said that she has really only one part, that of ' the Dance ' itself.

"*Mademoiselle Kyasht has now for five years upheld the purest traditions of ballet dancing in London, without even a momentary concession to the whims of popular taste, or the seductions of æsthetic crazes.*

"To dance as she has done night after night, with the rarest of holidays, can have been no light task. Its performance has also involved, we venture to think, a certain moral determination.

"The last five years, since the law opened the variety theatre to the *revue* and the vaudeville, have been difficult ones for the ballet in England. There came a time when it ceased to be the central feature of the programme at the Empire. Undeterred, Mademoiselle Kyasht became her own ballet mistress, and continued at last to present such exquisite trifles as 'The Water Nymph,' 'First Love,' and 'The Reaper's Dream.'

"There is pleasure, however, in the thought that her farewell has been taken in a more stately type of ballet, her Titania adapted from 'The Midsummer Night's Dream.' There is appropriateness in this, for she has during her stay in London almost made good Titania's own promise, hand in hand she has said to her partners :—

"'Hand in hand with fairy grace
Will *we dance* and bless this place.'

"Admirers of her art may find a crumb of consolation for her departure in the fact that we shall not need this time to go to Russia for the repair of our loss. If we may trust the statement that Miss Phyllis Bedells is to inherit her place, we shall soon have the rare satisfaction of watching an English *Première* at the Empire. In welcoming her, we shall welcome a dancer of tested worth, a practised mime, and what is more, a gay and sympathetic personality.

"We have regret for the queen who is abdicating, but we have faith in the queen who succeeds her."

On the opposite page is a photograph of me bidding farewell to my friends at the London station before setting off for New York. My partner, Litavkin, of whose tragedy I have previously written, is standing beside me. He accompanied me to the United States. When we arrived in New York we found the town placarded with posters about me, on which were printed : "Lydia Kyasht—The Talk of the Town."

From morning to night I was pestered with press representatives. They descended on me in massed attacks and asked me the most intimate questions, most of which it was utterly impossible to answer. When I had nothing more to tell them, they simply invented stories themselves about me. The most ridiculous of these was the one that declared I always walked upon my hands when not dancing in order to rest my feet. The result of this elaborate invention was that whenever

FAREWELL TO ENGLAND: Madame Lydia Kyasht starts for America in 1914. Beside her is her dancing partner, Litavkin, who later came to such a tragic end.

MY AMERICAN EXPERIENCES 181

I accepted an invitation anywhere people expected to see me walk upside down into their room. They appeared extremely disappointed, not to say cheated, to see me assume the usual perpendicular.

My salary was higher in America. They paid me one thousand seven hundred and fifty dollars a week. But the work was much harder than it had been at the Empire. I had to put in altogether nine performances during the week, including one on the Sunday.

My husband and I stayed at Claridge's Hotel. I was so tired out that I used to rest as much as possible during the day. We met a number of well-known Americans while we were over there. Among them was Mr. George Butler. He belonged to the famous Four Hundred, and was the head of the Pall Mall Cigarettes. One day he gave a big luncheon for me at one of the principal hotels. We had the most wonderful salads, and all kinds of American dishes that greatly intrigued me. Mr. Butler used to keep me regularly supplied with beautiful roses during my visit over there. As I love flowers I much appreciated this attention.

Another American millionaire, who was a friend of ours and a great habitué of the Empire, was Mr. S. A. Seligmann, commonly known as Fritz to his intimates. He had a charming house in London, situated in South Audley Street, and used to give parties there every Sunday which were very popular affairs indeed. He suffered from a slight lameness caused through having rescued a girl from a motor car, in the course of which he was himself crushed against a wall. Fritz was a stout man. He was enormously strong, and had very powerful muscles. But the thing that struck one most forcibly about him was his expressive-looking black eyes, and the fact that he was always smiling. I told him once, " If I feel depressed at any time I shall just send for you in order to look in your eyes, because they are so brimful of life and fun that they will drive away anybody's depression."

I have previously mentioned the persistence of the American press representatives. After my arrival in the States one of the Sunday papers photographed me in a group with several of the leading American millionaires. The paper paid a large sum for the exclusive rights of publication, but not, unfortunately, to me.

I took over some beautiful dresses which had been especially designed for me by Lucille (Lady Duff Gordon). Most of them were pure white, and without any colour at all on them.

We had a very trying time with the Customs about my professional wardrobe. They refused at first to pass my dresses through, saying I must have my stage clothes made in America. At length we managed to obtain possession of them by paying down a deposit of one hundred and fifty pounds, on the understanding that the money would be returned to us when my engagement was over at the Winter Garden Theatre. When the time arrived, however, to reclaim the deposit, the authorities refused to hand it over. In the end we were obliged to sail for England without it, and did not get it back until a considerable time had elapsed, and an interchange of acrimonious correspondence had taken place.

Lopokova was in America at the same time as me. She was appearing in one of the Cabarets there. I had not seen much of her hitherto as she became a pupil at the Imperial Ballet School two years after I commenced studying there.

According to the rule of the school every pupil had to wear her hair in two plaits irrespective of whether she had a sufficient quantity, or not, for the purpose. Lopokova had even less hair than Karsavina and I. To be exact she had altogether about six hairs, and I shall never forget my first glimpse of her with her two skimpy little pigtails, of about four inches in length, sticking out on either side of her head. As a child she used to act a good deal in the Imperial School.

Another famous person whom I met while I was in New York was Gaby Deslys. It was four years since a reigning King was reported to have lost his throne because of his devotion to her, and since he had made a hurried exit from his country. I could well understand when I saw her the power of her fascination over men. I thought her one of the most attractive women I had ever met. She had lovely blue eyes, rounded like enormous saucers, and a pair of the most perfectly modelled arms that would have delighted the eyes of a sculptor. Her partner, Harry Pilcer, was with her when we met. But she seemed chiefly preoccupied with a small Japanese dog, and all her admirers, of whom she had a score, took only a secondary place as compared to her regard for the little toy terrier.

I also met Mrs. Vernon Castle in America dancing at a cabaret. She looked very lovely indeed. At this particular cabaret the changing lighting had been introduced, with great effect as concerned the general scene and its picturesqueness.

Mr. Shubert had engaged me for six months, until I was due to appear at the Coliseum in July. But unfortunately, after I had only been playing three months, I contracted typhoid fever and was so seriously ill with it that I was obliged to cancel the rest of my American engagements. The Americans were very good to me, and entertained my husband and me a great deal until my unfortunate illness prevented us from accepting any further invitations. After I was strong enough I was sent away to the Lakewood Sanatorium to convalesce for six weeks.

A rich millionaire banker, Mr. Kenneth Cowan, was a great friend of ours. We used to meet also in London. One day after he had lunched with us at the Carlton, I suggested taking him to my clairvoyant to have his fortune told. (I have previously mentioned her correct reading of my lawsuit.) He pooh-poohed the idea of there being anything in clairvoyancy but eventually agreed to come all the same. When we arrived at her house she asked if he would prefer to be alone during his reading. But he told her he did not mind anybody being present in the least, much to my relief, as I badly wanted to hear what she had to say. Mr. Cowan gave her a ring to hold which he had been wearing. She placed it against her forehead, and leant back in her chair. Everybody waited expectantly, except Mr. Cowan himself, who looked rather bored with the whole proceedings. His expression soon changed when she told him: "You are married, but very unhappily. Your wife is in a mad-house. You yourself like a gay life and have a family in Paris. But *not by your wife.*" At this stage in the reading Mr. Cowan snatched the ring from her hand, and hurriedly left the room.

This particular clairvoyant was, as I have said before, a remarkable woman. Prior to going to America I consulted her about my trip. She warned me to be careful over the contract, or I should be swindled. Acting on her advice I showed the papers to my solicitors, and they altered various clauses in them which, if allowed to remain as framed, might have proved very awkward for me under certain circumstances. This clairvoyant also warned me of my illness, but told me I should eventually recover. To people who scoff about clairvoyancy one can only say that one cannot pierce the veil entirely, and that one does not wish to do so. But may not one be permitted an occasional lifting of the hem of it?

CHAPTER 20

STORIES OF KING EDWARD AND QUEEN ALEXANDRA

King Edward's favourite dance—An order from the management—When the King made an unexpected visit to the Empire—Command performances of the ballet—When the King fell asleep—Meetings with King Edward at the home of the Russian Ambassador—The latter's cure for asthma—Lord and Lady Walsingham give a party at Merton Hall—My first meeting with Queen Alexandra—My fatal curtsey—The Queen makes inquiries concerning an intimate undergarment—Lady Cheylesmore in an impromptu race, and a tearful scene—Pre-war parties in London.

HAVING danced before Royalty so frequently at the Imperial Ballet, I was naturally very anxious when I came over to England to dance before King Edward. I was delighted to learn that His Majesty was fond of going to theatres and music halls, and also that some form of entertainment was generally provided to amuse him by those hostesses who were honoured with his presence at their parties. They usually engaged well-known professionals whose names had been submitted to and approved by His Majesty. As I have previously explained, at my first appearance at the Empire before I took part in the Revue, the management put me on in a solo dance. For this number I wore my national costume, and the elaborate beaded and be-jewelled head-dress that went with it. When a well-known hostess invited me to dance at a party of hers to which King Edward was going, I decided to give this particular dance. His Majesty was so delighted with it that

EDWARD AND ALEXANDRA

I had to perform it afterwards at every party I went to at which he was present, while the management of the Empire also gave me instructions to dance it whenever he was in the theatre. This order led to considerable confusion on more than one occasion, as far as I personally was concerned, as no matter what number I might be billed to appear in, the instant King Edward was seen in the Royal Box, the Russian dance had to be immediately substituted. One evening he arrived quite unheralded. The sight of him in the Royal Box so excited me that I found to my horror I had completely forgotten the opening steps of his favourite dance.

Command performances of the ballet used to be held at the Castle for King Edward and Queen Alexandra. One of them was given prior to my arrival at which Madame Adeline Genée was commanded to appear. Mr. Cuthbert Clarke received instructions to take his orchestra and accompany her number. The performance was completed without a hitch. But whether the music which had been selected happened to be extra soothing in its timbre or not, I cannot say. At any rate, when the lights were raised at the end of the show, King Edward was discovered to be slumbering peacefully in his arm-chair.

The King was a great friend of the Russian Ambassador, and used to go to his house for bridge parties. I met him there on several occasions. One reason why he so enjoyed playing bridge there was because the Ambassador was a fellow-sufferer from asthma, and had discovered an excellent antidote of which the King always made use when he went there. This enabled him to enjoy his game in peace secure in the knowledge that, if a London fog crept up, there was a remedy at hand to ward off the subsequent attack of asthma. I often thought how he must have suffered in London in the winter, for as smokeless fuel was little in use then, the fogs were even worse then than they are now.

Among other personal friends of King Edward and Queen Alexandra whom I knew were Lord and Lady Walsingham. He was the sixth Baron, and had acted as a Lord-in-Waiting to Queen Victoria, so that his association with the Court went back for some while. Lady Walsingham was his second wife and was a charming and noted hostess. Both she and her husband gave some marvellous parties down at their country estate, Merton Hall, in Norfolk. I always looked forward to going to them. They were very interested in antiques, and possessed a valuable collection of *objets d'art*, all of which were displayed about the house, either in cabinets or on various little tables.

One day Lady Walsingham asked me to go down and dance at a party which she was giving, and which was to be honoured with the presence of Queen Alexandra. Until then I had not met the Queen, or danced before her, and felt tremendously excited at the prospect of doing so. My hostess took me across and presented me. When I made my curtsey I was so excited that I never observed a small table behind me loaded with precious curios. In rising from the ground I backed into it and upset the whole thing, scattering its contents in every direction. The Queen observed my action, and with a kindly wish to stop me in time, and preserve my hostess's household gods from damage, called out : " Take care ! " But her well-meant remark only increased my confusion. Happily, no material damage was done to Lady Walsingham's treasures, and the only sufferer from the accident appeared to be myself and the damage inflicted on my own self-esteem. I began to feel myself the victim of a malignant fairy, because whenever I wished to make a particularly good impression on anybody an accident always occurred, or else I transgressed in some other way equally distressing.

As most people are aware, Queen Alexandra suffered from deafness. This made it necessary to raise one's voice when speaking to Her Majesty, and awkward situations sometimes arose in consequence. I remember being an unwilling participant myself in such an incident. The hostess was again Lady Walsingham, and she had given an evening party which both the King and Queen had attended, and at which I had been dancing. When I had finished my solo Queen Alexandra sent for me. I hastened to obey the Royal summons, expecting to receive some congratulations on my dancing. Instead Her Majesty inquired, in tones which could be heard the length and breadth of the crowded reception room : *" Tell me, Mademoiselle Kyasht, do you wear corsets when you dance ? "*

My embarrassment can be better imagined than described, since those were the demure days when such articles of apparel were never given a public mention, and when women encased their long-suffering limbs within marvellous structures of steel and whalebone. It followed, therefore, that when I meekly informed the Queen I never wore corsets she regarded me with astonishment, and expressed great surprise at my being able to manage without them. Meanwhile all the guests were perforce embarrassed and unwilling listeners to our conversation since, owing to the Queen's deafness, it had to be pitched in tones that penetrated to every corner of the room. In the midst of my own confusion I yet derived some pleasure at the sight of their pink cheeks and flurried gestures, and the obvious manner in which all of them tried themselves to cultivate a sudden fit of deafness.

When I was at the Empire I used to be inundated with requests to accept engagements to dance at private parties throughout the London season until I became quite surfeited with them, and refused to accept any that did not appeal to me and were not given by hostesses whom I knew personally. I remember accepting one for a party which Lady Cheylesmore was holding at her house at Prince's Gate, and which was to be attended by Queen Alexandra, and other members of the Royal Family. Under such circumstances as these, I was naturally anxious to give as perfect a performance as possible. Almost my first thought was who should accompany me on the piano? Lady Cheylesmore explained she had a very celebrated lady pianist taking part in the programme, and suggested it would be a novel idea if she accompanied me. Personally I felt rather nervous at the prospect of being assisted in this respect by a total stranger, however capable she might be. I put forward the alternative suggestion, therefore, that the pair of us should have a preliminary rehearsal beforehand. But the lady pianist absolutely vetoed this, and declared it was quite unnecessary. So against my better judgment I yielded the point.

When it was my turn to appear on the night of the party I started gaily off with the opening steps of my solo, and was promptly pulled up by the discovery that my steps were not agreeing with the *tempo* of the music. I stopped, and intimated as politely as possible to my accompanist that both of us should commence again from the beginning. She looked annoyed at the idea, but complied. We started off once more but the second attempt also proved an utter failure. Her *tempo* and my steps refused to agree at all, and she was still at the top of the page of her musical score when I had already reached the bottom. At last I realized the impossibility of dancing at all to her accompaniment, and refused to continue any longer. She was very indignant at my decision and a distressing scene followed, in the course of which each of us sought to blame the other for our failure. It terminated in us both dissolving into tears in the full view of all the guests. And what was infinitely worse in front of Queen Alexandra. What Her Majesty thought of such behaviour I cannot imagine. But after that, whenever anybody asked me to dance at a private party, I either insisted on taking my own accompanist along with me, or else having a rehearsal beforehand.

In those pre-war days dancing had not reached the craze it has now, when it absorbs the whole evening, and musical receptions were a great feature of the parties then. This was all to the good as far as artistes were concerned, as it provided them with an additional source of income, besides enlarging the scope of their audience. One wonders whether artistes of to-day have gained so much from their increased salaries as they think, since when King Edward and Queen Alexandra were reigning there was a great spirit of *bonhomie*. Artistes exerted themselves to give of their best not only because of the pecuniary rewards attached to their engagements, but because of their desire to make an artistic success. At the present time it seems to me that a number of people give first place to the dollars, and last place to the art, instead of placing art first of all.

CHAPTER 21

CELEBRITIES I HAVE KNOWN

My first English party—Sir Austin and Lady Harris—A comedy of errors—Mutual explanations—Lord and Lady Lonsdale—Our first meeting—Lord Lonsdale in a new rôle as a French scholar—Britain declares War on Germany— In Vienna—" Les Sylphides "—Dancing with Nijinsky— A quarrel—At Lowther Castle during war time—Lady Lonsdale and I have a neck-to-neck race—A great friend— Mr. Gordon Selfridge—Sir Thomas Lipton—My " faux pas "—A story concerning a " faux pas " by somebody else—Why Madame Adeline Genée drank no wine—An autocratic ballerina—Stories of Genée—When she refused six hundred a week.

WHEN I came over to England in 1908 the majority of English people regarded Russia as a savage sort of uncivilized country where bears were allowed to roam at large, and where the people themselves were little better than barbarians. Thus it came about that I had some amusing experiences. I shall never forget the first house party I went to in England. My host and hostess were Sir Austin and Lady Harris, and they invited me to spend the week-end with them at their country place in Hampshire. He was the Deputy-Chairman of Lloyd's Bank, and was at one time associated with the Board of Contracts at the War Office.

Owing to its being my first visit to England I did not know any of the social customs, and as Russians did not wear full evening dress to informal parties, it never occurred to me to pack one. So my wardrobe was extremely scanty, and included only a coat and skirt and a semi-evening dress.

On arriving at the Harris's country place the butler showed me into the garden. There I experienced my first surprise, for I found my hostess dressed in a black ballet costume and performing a solo dance on the lawn. The sight astonished me, but I was charmed to think that such a delightful custom prevailed at English country house parties, and considered Lady Harris was the most beautiful creature I had seen since my arrival in England. It transpired later that she had really dressed in this fashion from a wish to honour me and show me that English people were interested in the ballet and its progress. But at the time, of course, I was unaware of this, and only thought to myself—" Other countries, other customs."

After a while the butler announced that luncheon was served, and everybody went indoors. There a second surprise awaited me, for, instead of the guests seating themselves at a table, they all sat cross-legged upon the floor. By this time I was feeling slightly bewildered. But imagining this to be another queer custom of the English people, I copied my fellow-guests' example and sat cross-legged too. Then came my third and last surprise. The butler, wearing an air of great solemnity, proceeded to pass round a silver mug filled with *vodka*. It was handed from one guest to another, and each of them in turn sipped its contents. When it came to my turn I did not like to refuse, although privately it occurred to me as being a somewhat unsanitary habit, and one likely to promote colds

A GREAT SPORTSMAN: THE EARL OF LONSDALE.

A snapshot of Lord Lonsdale at home at Lowther Castle, taken by Madame Lydia Kyasht during one of her visits there.

CELEBRITIES I HAVE KNOWN 195

if not other and worse ailments. Conversation was necessarily somewhat limited during luncheon, as far as I was concerned, owing to my ignorance of the language. I was delighted to discover that one of the guests had had the forethought to come prepared with a Franco-Russian dictionary, and was able to act as an interpreter of sorts on my behalf. After a while I began to wonder what was the matter with my fellow-guests. They looked so miserable, and judging from their expressions, appeared to be in the depths of discomfort. However, I was soon to be enlightened. Presently one of them leant towards me, and enquired in halting French : " *Are you not surprised, Mademoiselle Kyasht, to find that we know all your Russian customs, and can behave just like Russians do ?* "

Mutual explanations ensued. It transpired that they all had been making martyrs of themselves for my sake, under the mistaken impression that my country people always sat down crosslegged to meals, and drank *vodka* from a communal mug. They were all greatly relieved to learn that there was no need for them to sacrifice themselves in such a fashion. For the remainder of my visit everybody deserted the floor, and thankfully occupied a chair. Since those days I have made many English friends, and enjoyed many parties. But my first will always linger in my memory as being the most unique.

Lord and Lady Lonsdale are both friends of my husband and I. On the opposite page is a snapshot of Lord Lonsdale which I took when I was staying with him and his wife at Lowther Castle. The first time I met him was when he was arranging a charity performance in aid of the Charing Cross Hospital, at which I was dancing. All the artistes who had taken part were invited to a big supper party after the entertainment was over. Of course I went. I had been wearing a red wig with my dance costume, and when Lord Lonsdale saw me in evening dress and with a diamond tiara upon my head, he did not recognize me and asked who I was. My English was still extremely poor, and his French was not much better. But we contrived to make ourselves understood. Shortly afterwards I sailed to America, and we did not meet again until my return, when he came to the Coliseum several times to watch me dance.

Neither my husband nor I had had much opportunity of studying the English country places, so we were delighted to receive an invitation to stay at Lowther Castle, and looked forward to seeing the Lake scenery of which we had heard so much. We found the castle beautiful and the surrounding country glorious. An atmosphere of peace seemed to brood over everything. But the quiet of those August days was rudely shattered by the bombshell of war. On August 1st Germany declared war against Russia, and on the 4th Great Britain declared war against Germany. My husband and I had experienced so many revolutions that war held a far more poignant message for us than it did for those fortunate people who had always led peaceful sheltered lives. We realized the full horror of it.

It was with many inward misgivings indeed that I bade farewell to my husband a few days later, when he set off on his journey to Russia to join his regiment. Lord and Lady Lonsdale cheered my loneliness by offering me a home with them for a while. So I stayed on at Lowther Castle until the unexpected suicide of my dancing partner, Litavkin, compelled me to leave them in order to find another partner to take his place.

Just before war was declared I had been fulfilling a dancing engagement in Vienna. The Austrians were very embittered against the Russians, and ready to pick a quarrel on the slightest provocation. Diaghileff was staging the ballet, "Les Sylphides," and in it Nijinsky was my dance partner. I had known Nijinsky for some years, as we had danced together in the Imperial Ballet. He made his first appearance as a *premier danseur* with me in a ballet entitled "Pahica." When we were dancing together in Vienna he was very moody, and not in the least like his usual self. One evening he grumbled at me so much that when the audience demanded an encore I refused to dance it with him, and told him to find somebody else in the cast to take my place. At last Diaghileff came on the stage himself in order to ascertain what was the matter between us. I told him how Nijinsky had been behaving, and how he had upset me by making unkind remarks the whole time we had been dancing our *pas deux*, and that it was impossible to continue dancing with him under such circumstances. Diaghileff was very kind indeed, and asked me as a personal favour to dance the encore. I agreed to do so. He was alive to the intense importance of keeping our Viennese audience in a good humour. They were already getting out of hand and beginning to shout and display equally vehement signs of anger at being kept so long waiting. I must admit, on that particular occasion I was not altogether sorry to say good-bye to Vienna.

I stayed at Lowther Castle again later on in the war, during one of their shooting parties. Lady Lonsdale, who is an expert knitter, tried to teach me how to knit socks for the soldiers. I am afraid I dropped more stitches than I purled at first. My hostess possessed great patience and refused to despair. In the end her efforts were successful, and I became quite a creditable knitter. She was over sixty then, but one of the most active women I have ever met. She was busy from morning to night.

We used to go and lunch with the guns, and would ride to and fro there on ponies. Unlike my hostess, I was a very indifferent rider, and my ballet poise quite forsook me whenever I sat on a horse. One day Lady Lonsdale's pony suddenly took it into its head to gallop. Mine promptly followed suit until my hostess and I were riding a species of neck-to-neck race. I was terrified. Flinging both arms around my pony's neck I screamed with fright—an act which naturally enough caused him to gallop all the faster. In the end one of the grooms came to my rescue. But for the remainder of my visit I absolutely refused to mount another pony.

Another great friend of ours is Mr. Gordon Selfridge. He is godfather to our little girl Pouffée. Her other godparents are Madame Adeline Genée and Pavlova. Most American business men are hard workers, and Mr. Selfridge certainly belongs to this category. I always tell him that work is his hobby because he never does anything else. As a matter of fact, he indulges sometimes in a game of poker. When he comes to our house to play we always make him eat a real Russian supper. He does not dislike Russian cooking, or find it in the least too rich. It was Mr. Gordon Selfridge who introduced Sir Thomas Lipton to me. We were at a party together, and he told me a friend of his wanted to meet me, and brought Sir Thomas across. In my own mind Sir Thomas Lipton and tea were indissolubly associated, with the result that I held out my hand to him, and exclaimed to everybody's amazement, " How do you do, Sir Thomas Lipton-Tea ? " Mr. Selfridge roared with laughter at my *faux pas*. But as Sir Thomas forgave me, everything was all right.

I am not the only person who commits *faux pas*, however, and I remember overhearing a most amusing one once when I was dining with some friends at a West-end restaurant. Near us was a table occupied by a very pretty girl and a young man. Presently I heard her asking him, " Is it really true that we are going to have the freedom of the sea ? " He looked rather puzzled and inquired her reason for being interested in the subject, whereupon she made the surprising retort, " Because it affects me personally, of course. Last summer I was staying at B——, and the stupid local authorities refused to let one bathe where one pleased, but restricted bathers to certain portions of the beach where there were no spectators. This year I have bought a fascinating new bathing suit, and so, of course, I want the freedom of the sea in which to show it ! " Her escort appeared too astonished at this original point of view to have any reply ready, so took refuge in silence instead.

Ballet dancers have to be very abstemious in

their habits, and Madame Adeline Genée would never drink wine on this account because she considered it would interfere with her dancing. I believe she only broke this rule once, and that was at a luncheon party in her own home, at which she drank half a glass of wine to please her husband.

Probably no two dancers could be more unlike temperamentally than Madame Genée and myself. She was at the Empire altogether for about fourteen years, and became somewhat of an autocrat, and inclined to assume the rights of absolute sovereignty. Once Mr. Cuthbert Clarke, the musical director, incurred her displeasure. Notice had been given that an important personage was occupying a box that evening, and Mr. Clarke bestowed a fleeting glance upwards to see if he was there. When the performance was over a message was delivered requesting Mr. Clarke to go round to Madame Genée's dressing-room. He went and found an indignant *ballerina*. " I expect you to look only at me when I am on the stage, Mr. Clarke, and not to glance at the occupier of one of the boxes, no matter what his rank may be," she admonished him in icy accents. " Kindly bear that in mind in the future." That is only one side of Madame Adeline Genée, and not the most important one, as she is a delightfully attractive person and a fascinating friend.

The directors of the Empire Theatre gave a big dinner to celebrate the tenth anniversary of her engagement. Genée's husband, Mr. Isitt, was present, and also her father and mother. Her parents were very proud of their famous daughter and her achievements. She really gave up her dancing in the end because of her husband, though the reason she left the Empire was because they would not pay her the salary for which she asked. It is not to be supposed from that action of hers that she put money before her art, because she did nothing of the sort, as the following story illustrates. She was touring the provinces, and had engaged Mr. Cuthbert Clarke to accompany her with his orchestra. At one town they visited a man introduced himself to Mr. Clarke, and mistaking the latter for her business manager invited him to fix up a week at six hundred pounds at the Theatre Royal at Glasgow. Mr. Clarke suggested that it would be best to approach personally Madame Adeline Genée. But the other declared his preference for an intermediary. Somewhat reluctantly Mr. Clarke agreed to put the proposition forward, although he candidly admitted beforehand that he did not think Madame Genée would agree to it for a single instant. He was quite correct about her attitude. When the offer was put to her she made a grimace, and retorted, " I would not go there if they gave me the theatre, and a thousand pounds a week as well!" And no argument would induce her to change her mind.

Undoubtedly it was due to the genius of Madame Genée that the Empire became recognized as the home of ballet, just as it was she who was also responsible, to a great extent, for the standard of ballet dancing being raised in England. Yet, like many other pioneers in different fields she has suffered from the fact that she has sown the seeds for others to reap the harvest. Many people held the opinion that she did not receive the monetary reward her ability deserved and to which she was entitled while she was at the Empire.

CHAPTER 22

FAMOUS BEAUTIES OF THE PAST, AND THE PRESENT

A beautiful Princess—Princess Belosselsky-Belozersky—Aide-de-Camp to the Tsar—A nickname—A Princess who spent ten thousand per annum on her clothes—The Countess who lost her knickers—Beauty and make-up—My little daughter is born—Her christening—Stories about Pouffée —Her adventures with a fish—The Beauty of the Court— A " golden " accident —" The most beautiful girl in England "—Lady Diana Duff-Cooper—Society debutantes want to learn the dance King Edward liked—The only girl in London who succeeded in doing so—My opinion of what makes a beautiful woman.

EVERY nation has its own standard of beauty, and each type makes its own individual appeal. The Russian Court was noted for its beautiful women. They were a most distinctive type, with their sapphire-blue eyes and beautiful glossy black hair. One in particular, Princess Belosselsky-Belozersky—the wife of Prince Orloff—was so exceptionally good-looking that, whenever she drove through the streets of St. Petersburg, people would stand still to watch her and would call to one another, " Ah, look ! The beautiful Princess is coming ! " Her husband was Aide-de-Camp to the Tsar, and earned the disapproval of the Tsarina because he openly avowed dislike of her favourite, Rasputin. He was very popular, all the same, with the Emperor, and was given the nickname of " The chauffeur of the Tsar," because he used to drive the Tsar about a great deal in his car. His wife, Princess Belosselsky-Belozersky, was fabulously wealthy and was commonly reputed to spend ten thousand pounds a year on her clothes. Certainly she was always exquisitely dressed. Her colouring and style are English, as she has blue eyes and a tall graceful figure. Naturally she had any number of admirers in Russia, and was besides one of the most prominent hostesses in St. Petersburg. Before her marriage she used to be a desperate little flirt. So much so that it was reported she even flirted with the Imperial pages. But, as I have previously explained, the latter were by no means inexperienced lads. The Princess took a great interest in the Imperial Ballet, and often came to see me dance at the Opera House. One year she was staying at Wiesbaden at the same time as I, and so we became acquainted and used to play bridge together every afternoon—of which game both of us were very fond.

Another woman at the Imperial Court who had the reputation of being well dressed was the Countess Nieroth, whose husband was attached to the Tsar's *entourage*. There was a most amusing story circulated about her. One day she was walking across to the Winter Palace, accompanied by an officer of the Second Life Guards, and she suddenly felt something descending. Looking down she discovered her knickers were lying around her ankles. Her presence of mind did not desert her in this trying predicament. Turning towards the officer as if nothing out of the ordinary had happened, she said, " Please go on ahead of me, and do not turn round ! " As soon as he had left her she stooped down, pulled off her knickers, and, rolling them up into a bundle, tucked them under her arm and rejoined him.

Somebody asked me once whether I thought English women dressed well. Personally, I think they manage to achieve smartness without sacrificing a certain quietness in their attire which, as far as they are concerned, is a hallmark. For example, one can always tell a Jewess at sight because of her love of bright colours. It is the same with the Italians and the Viennese. Another advantage the English woman possesses is her fresh complexion. She does not have to make up unless she wishes to, whereas the French woman is sometimes obliged to do so in order to camouflage the sallowness of her skin, and the final result is anything but becoming. It is odd that so many people will not grasp the important fact that make-up should be used to enhance beauty, and never for the purpose of concealing blemishes. As for the short skirts one hears so much about, one must admit that they are both smart and practical, and infinitely more sensible than the trailing atrocities which were affected in the 'nineties.

The year 1921 was a momentous one for me because my little girl was born on June 28th. Pouffée was christened at the Russian Ambassador Church in London. On the opposite page is a picture of the ceremony, and of the priest wearing his ceremonial robes. Pavlova, who was one of our baby's godparents, is holding her in her arms, while Mr. Gordon Selfridge is standing beside her and Madame Adeline Genée beyond. Russian parents give very careful study to the question of who shall be invited to act as their child's godparents. My husband and I gave a great deal of thought as to whom we should invite to become sponsors for Lydia the Second, for she was

AT THE CHRISTENING OF MADAME LYDIA KYASHT'S LITTLE DAUGHTER
IN THE RUSSIAN AMBASSADOR CHURCH, 1921.

Left to right : The baby's nurse, and her godparents, Madame Pavlova (holding the baby), Mr. Gordon Selfridge and Madame Adeline Genée.

christened after me. We asked Madame Pavlova and Madame Genée to act as her godmothers because we believed that she would gain talent and inspiration for dancing from them, and we askəd Mr. Gorden Selfridge to be her godfather because we thought she would gain intelligence from him. He is very fond of her, and calls her his " Precious Stone."

From the time Pouffée could toddle she has taken an interest in dancing, and has already made up her mind to become a *ballerina*. When she was quite tiny she took part in an amateur production in London in aid of a charity, and very much amused the audience by stopping in the middle of the stage and exclaiming at the top of her voice, " That's my mummie dancing there ! " On another occasion she was sitting in the front of the stalls watching me in one of my ballets. In the course of my solo I had to scatter flowers about the stage. Lydia watched me doing this until her sense of tidiness became too much for her, and she called out, " Stop dancing, Mummie ! Stop dancing, and pick up the pitty flowers ! " This aside quite spoilt the dance, although it supplied a human touch that very much intrigued the audience, who did not even know I was married.

My little daughter certainly inherits my mischievous ways, for she is up to all sorts of pranks. Once she was ill in a nursing home, and nearly frightened the life out of her nurse by making her think she had fallen over the balcony into the street below. The nurse had left her by herself for a second, and Pouffée promptly seized the opportunity to jump out of bed and try and catch a little bird that had perched on the balcony rail.

While she was so occupied the nurse returned, and could not imagine where Pouffée had gone. Having searched everywhere in vain, even to looking under the bed and inside the wardrobe, she rushed to the balcony expecting to find some appalling tragedy had been enacted in her absence, instead of which she found Pouffée calmly seated enjoying her discomfiture. Pouffée was sent to bed supperless as a punishment, and ever since then has held a poor opinion of the catering qualities of a nursing home. But she deserved it really for giving everybody such a fright, apart from the fact that she might have made herself much worse. When Pouffée is in a serious mood she is as solemn as a judge, but sometimes she is the personification of Puck. I shall always remember my husband and me being photographed after her christening. I carried Pouffée, a small bundle wrapped in a shawl, in my arms.

When she was five years old she went to stay at the seaside. One day she was fishing from a break-water, and succeeded in getting a bite the strength of which pulled her into the water. Instead of being frightened at this, she calmly let go of the fish and, scrambling ashore, proceeded homewards, where she put herself to bed as a punishment, because—as she quaintly explained afterwards—" I was not really supposed to go in the sea, you know!"

I look forward to some future day when Lydia the Second will follow in her mother's footsteps, and uphold the traditions of the Imperial Ballet.

The most outstanding personality at the Imperial Court was undoubtedly Wyrubova. In her younger days she was known as " The Beauty of the Court." The description was certainly apt when she was dressed in her full Court robes, for at such times she looked really exquisite. She was dark-haired and had a pair of magnificent black-brown eyes above a retroussé-shaped nose. From my personal recollection of her I should say that she was an exact type of what Elinor Glyn has immortalized to this generation as "*IT* "!— because Wyrubova was brimful of this particular quality from her head to her toes. Owing to her influence over the Tsarina she possessed tremendous power at Court, and her word and influence carried far.

I remember a particular incident that occurred which illustrated how she could turn everything, even an accident, to her personal advantage. She had been travelling by train to Petrograd, and an accident occurred on the line in the course of which she suffered an injury to her leg. When the news of this disaster was conveyed to the Tsarina, she promptly enlisted the sympathy of the Tsar, and to such good purpose that he ordered the Railway Company to pay Wyrubova a huge sum of money by way of compensation for the injury to her leg. They were obliged to comply with the Imperial demand. This liberality caused considerable ill feeling among others who were less fortunate, and it was generally remarked—" That Wyrubova had had a *golden accident.*"

When I first came to England I was told many stories concerning the beautiful Lady Diana Manners, the daughter of the Duke of Rutland, and who is married now to Captain Duff-Cooper. We had heard her beauty spoken of over in Russia.

And she was reported to be " the most beautiful girl in England." Naturally this statement fired me with a desire to see her and judge for myself whether this was true. Our meeting came about in a curious way. My correspondence was increasing daily, what with invitations to dance and go to parties, to have my photograph taken, to sign my autograph, to tell parents whether their daughter should take up ballet dancing as a career, and countless other requests of a similarly tiresome nature. I told my husband that as he made a habit of opening my correspondence it was only fair he should answer the letters, and turned the whole batch over to him to grapple with as best he could. It had spread abroad how much King Edward liked my Russian dance. The result was that I was inundated with requests from well-known society women begging me to teach it to them. What would have happened had I acceded to all the requests made I cannot imagine. One may assume that the King would have been entertained for some years to come with replicas of my dance at every party he attended. One day Lady Diana Manners made the same request to me, and being curious to meet her, I arranged an interview. The meeting proved to be my own undoing, for she was too beautiful to refuse anything to, and so she became the only girl in London to whom I taught the Russian dance. Whether she ever danced it herself afterwards to King Edward I never heard. But I do know that she looked most attractive rehearsing, and that as I watched her, clad in a short practice tunic that displayed all her contours, I said to myself, " What a lovely body ! "

FAMOUS BEAUTIES

Personally I believe in the policy adopted by the ancient Greeks. They were beauty lovers in the truest sense of the word because they regarded their bodies in the light of a temple to be kept in a state of perpetual fitness and vigour, and paid as much attention to the development of their limbs as to the perfection of their profile. At one period people were so narrow-minded that they would have blushed at any mention of the body. They regarded any allusion to it as indelicate, preferring to assume that one lived and breathed from one's head. To-day they have learnt that such an attitude is mock modesty and ridiculous, and that their bodies are *lent to them* to be made temporary use of and should be kept in health and vigour. The famous beauties of the past have never relied on their faces alone to gain them a reputation for beauty. Neither did the Greeks, who may be said to be the primary founders of physical culture, as well as of classical dancing. Take any nation that has gone in for dancing and it will be found that their women are lithe and graceful in build, and full of health. The Egyptian women are a case in point. Many Europeans have sought to copy their graceful carriage. Personally, I do not consider any woman can lay claim to the title of " beautiful " unless she has first mastered the rudiments of physical culture and learnt how to inhabit the temporary temple of her body.

CHAPTER 23

UNDER THE RED FLAG!

The all-powerful Checka—" Cat and Mouse Act "—My father-in-law—In the hands of the mob—Eternal sleep—My mother-in-law dies—Arrested—Secret Orders—Identified by a ring—Two famous Russian Generals—Their fate—Not a libertine — A fanatic — Revolution — General Korniloff—Betrayed — My husband is warned — Escape — A Contrast—The Bolshevist Creed—Practice and theory—A ghoulish incident—The fate of a well-known Russian millionaire—Subjected to the Third Degree—A cruel jest —A slavery of body and spirit.

In Russia at the present time conditions are a little better, and there are prospects opening out of a brighter future. Just after the commencement of the revolution the condition of affairs could only be compared to Hades. All the large houses were seized by the Government, who allowed the owners just one room to live in. One never knew when one was going to be searched, and one's personal belongings confiscated on the plea that the authorities must go through them for defamatory matter. This process appeared to last interminably, as the things were never returned.

If anybody was rash enough to express an adverse criticism concerning the prevailing condition of affairs, the speaker was promptly hauled before the *Checka*. This was a sort of Special Commission that had been set up, and which was invested with absolute authority. For example, if they chose to do so, they could order any prisoner to be shot without even waiting for the

UNDER THE RED FLAG!

formality of a trial. Or, alternatively, they could have them clapped into a cell and left to languish there indefinitely.

The practices employed by the Russian revolutionists were far more cruel than any employed during the French Revolution, because the *Checka* delighted in indulging in every form of mental torture which their ingenuity could devise. A favourite torment was subsequently christened by the victims the "Cat and Mouse Act." The procedure was to drag the unfortunate prisoner before the authorities and inform him that he would be shot at dawn. Then, after the victim had endured a night of mental torture, he would be told a counter order had come through—"Wait." Day after day this grimmest of "comedies" would be played, until the wretched prisoner was reduced to the verge of nervous prostration, if not actual madness. Generally, after undergoing twelve months of this sort of treatment, it came as a merciful release when the genuine order was given. Small wonder that under such circumstances even young men and women became white-haired and prematurely aged.

My husband and I lost all our possessions during the revolution. My own escape from my fatherland I will deal with later. But now I am dealing with the period when my father-in-law, General Alexander Nicholaevitch Ragosin, was still alive. He was a Lieutenant-General in the Russian Army. His family were very wealthy and had a large country estate, called Schtevetz, situated near Kursk, which was famous for its nightingales. It was worked and tilled by peasants who had lived on the land for generations past. When the revolution burst like a bombshell upon everybody, my father-in-law refused to leave his home. "My people know me," he said. "I have done no harm to anybody."

He was devoted to his wife, and it worried him exceedingly to witness the serious effect the revolution was having on her general health, and how it was affecting her heart. She, on her part, lived in daily dread of what the revolutionaries might do to *him*. Her fears in this respect were further heightened by an incident which occurred during the beginning of the revolution, when she and her husband were staying in the town of Kursk. Their house was in Town Square. One day they heard an appalling outcry. It was the mob, who had got out of hand. They had seized the General commanding the garrison and were dragging him along the street. They tore his clothes off him and forced him to dance in bare feet on pieces of jagged glass. When they tired of this form of "sport," they set him up as a human target and took pot shots at him. But they were careful only to wound, and not to kill outright. This incident, of which she was an eye-witness, seriously affected my mother-in-law's health; in fact, she never properly recovered from it.

Later, when they were back at Schtevetz, she went upstairs one day to her room to rest. Several hours elapsed, and as she had not awakened, her husband decided to rouse her. He found she had passed to her eternal sleep. After her death my father-in-law strenuously opposed all attempts to persuade him to leave Russia, declaring, "My wife is buried here. She did not desert me, and I will never desert her grave." He gave instructions that the houes was to be left exactly as it had been in her lifetime, and that nothing in the rooms was to be touched.

Although we were anxious about him, we did not imagine his life was in actual danger, since we regarded the previous incident rather as the action of an infuriated mob than an expression of animosity against any individual person. We were wrong, however. He was not destined to escape the fatal clutch of the Bolshevists. They arrested him, and took him away under escort to a village about thirty-five miles distant from his home. But things were not to be as easy for them as they had imagined. The first hitch occurred when the time came to prefer a charge against him. They did not know with what to charge him. He was not guilty of any crime, nor of any political offence. Under such circumstances the only thing they could do was to trump up a charge against him. They accused him of trying to suppress the revolution in Turkestan!

The news of his arrest filtered through to Moscow, and his friends there moved heaven and earth in their efforts to procure his release. He was eventually brought before the *Checka*, and he protested his innocence of the charge brought against him. They responded by ordering him back to his cell. At length, after many weary months, a friend succeeded in obtaining an order for his immediate release, but the Bolshevists were not to be so easily robbed of their prey in this fashion. They took instant action, and issued a secret and counter order—" *Release under cover, and shoot him quick!* "

My father-in-law was not more than fifty-eight years of age then. But sorrow combined with the strain he had undergone had prematurely aged him. In spite of all the indignities he had undergone, he sustained absolute faith that he would be eventually released; so when one morning the warder came to his cell and said, " General! Come with me," he was delighted, and hailing the man with joy, asked him, " Has my release come through?"

The warder was one of my father-in-law's own peasants. Perhaps—who knows?—some gleam of affection lingered yet in his memory, for he averted his eyes as he answered, " No, General. *You are to be killed!*"

We were told afterwards that my father-in-law asked the soldiers to make a good end of him. Their interpretation of this request, made by a man who had never harmed any of them, was to shoot him in both legs, and then, as he sank helpless to the earth, to riddle his fallen body with bullets. They flung him on a heap of other murdered men, and there he remained unburied for fourteen months.

How grim were the scenes of identification in those days! My father-in-law was subsequently identified by means of the gold signet ring on his little finger. This ring was afterwards forwarded to my husband by the friends who found it. I think it is his most treasured possession.

Two famous Russian Generals, who were friends of my father-in-law, were Ratko Dmitrieff and Rouzsky. Their fate was even worse than his. The Bolshevists buried the two unfortunate men right up to their necks in earth. Then, springing

UNDER THE RED FLAG! 215

on horseback, they rode past at the gallop and, as they swept by, drew their swords and deftly sliced off their heads.

As for the Grand Dukes and the Imperial family, their end is too well known to need repetition. The Grand Duke Serge and the Grand Duke Constantine Constantovitch and Prince Igor were all three assassinated. They were either killed outright, or else—worse fate still!—were flung into a pit and left there to linger in torture until death put an end to their sufferings. Had they been the extravagant-living libertines that some of the revolutionists made them out to be, they would still not have deserved such a fate. But as it was, their chief fault—if fault it could be called—lay in trusting the mob who betrayed them. Some people have called Lenin an idealist. Personally, I think fanatic is a far better term. He was the person responsible for what is known in history as the "October Revolution," and on his shoulders must rest the responsibility of having brought Russia so low.

My husband suffered an appalling experience at the hands of the Kerensky revolutionists and the Bolshevists, who engineered the second rising, after the fall of Kerensky, when the Lenin Government took the power in their hands. A fortnight after February 28th, 1917, when the Tsar had inspected the Imperial troops, the revolution was in full swing. My husband was acting as Second-in-Command of the Reserve Battalion of the Tsar's First Rifle Guard, and was chosen by the Revolutionary Council to act as Chief of the Garrison at Tsarskoe-Selo. By accepting this post he found himself in a position to assist several of his brother officers who were under arrest. The revolutionists held innumerable meetings, and were so successful in the beginning that *fifteen hundred out of six thousand* turned Bolshevists. Within the space of two months they had *three hundred* of their own followers in the Battalion itself. It was about this time that the Battalion decided to print its own newspaper. At first the scheduled programme was anti-Bolshevist. But, like everything else, it speedily changed its policy and became pro-Bolshevist, and a mouthpiece for the ideas and creed of Lenin and the rabid revolutionists.

General Korniloff was moved from the front to St. Petersburg to command the garrison there, and received instructions to take a high hand with the revolutionaries. The attempt to do so proved a failure, however, owing to Kerensky's betraying him. It seems to be a general trait of Bolshevism to seize every opportunity and to turn it to personal advantage. At any rate, this was the policy pursued by Lenin and his adherents on this particular occasion, for they warned their followers that the entire revolutionary movement was being endangered through General Korniloff. The result of this piece of strategy on their part was that thousands of the soldiers turned Bolshevists with the object of protecting themselves. Alexis was warned to remain in barracks, and a little while afterwards received a hint that it would be wiser of him to come over to England and join me. He went to St. Petersburg and when he got there found the Second Revolution in full swing and the entire garrison given over to the Bolshevists. It was unsafe even to walk about the streets, because of the continual skirmishing and firing that went on.

UNDER THE RED FLAG! 217

After considerable difficulty, my husband managed to get a little money changed by the Minister of Foreign Affairs. Having accomplished this he put up in a small hotel opposite the station, in order to be in readiness to seize the first opportunity of getting away. He had his passport ready. On it he was described as : " Russian-born citizen. Exempt from Service. Going to England on trade business." He would not leave his beloved uniform behind him, however, but carried it with him done up in a parcel, as well as a packet of important Government dispatches which he was empowered to deliver to the Russian Embassy in London.

One night, about three o'clock in the morning, Alexis was awakened by the sound of heavy footsteps and loud voices outside in the corridor. It proved to be a detachment of the Red Guards, searching for any escaping officers. They knocked twice on his door, and demanded admittance, but he made no reply. Presently he heard one of them asking the night porter, " Who occupies this room ? " The latter explained that "it was an Englishman, going to London." What magic lies in a name ! The mere word " Englishman " appeared sufficient to satisfy the Red Guards. After inquiring of the porter whether he had seen the visitor's papers, and receiving the satisfactory answer, " Yes. Everything is in order," off they went and continued their search elsewhere.

When my husband reached the frontier of Finland he experienced further delay, for all passports had to be inspected. Whether the police were suspicious of him or not, it is impossible to say ; but they retained his passport, and it was only by the use of much bad language and a display of muscle that he ultimately contrived to regain possession of it. He arrived at the station only just in time to board the train as it was gliding out.

When he arrived in London he was extremely astonished to find everything was going on as usual there, and the shops were full of goods awaiting purchasers. The contrast between the conditions prevailing in England and the misery prevalent throughout Russia was amazing to anybody coming fresh from the appalling experiences he had undergone. Theoretically the Bolshevist creed is that everybody is equal. But in actual practice it means *absolute despotism*. A particular incident that occurred during the Kerensky revolution foreshadowed this trait in a grim and ghoulish manner. A stout Quartermaster in one of the Guards regiments was so imprudent as to venture a complaint about the quality of the soup served to him. The soldiers decided to make an object lesson of him. They seized him, cut him up in small pieces, and flung his remains into the soup—in order, as they said, to flavour it. This story may sound far fetched, but it is true for all that.

I have already mentioned how cruel the *Checka* were. The following incident sheds further light on some of their methods of dealing with prisoners. A friend of ours, a Russian millionaire, was hauled up before this " Tribunal of Justice " and accused of having sent money to the White Army, who had been fighting the Bolshevists in Southern Russia. He assured them he had done nothing of the sort, but they refused to accept his assurance, and said, " Your cashier went south, and then disappeared."

Goaded by this, the millionaire retorted, " Yes, he disappeared because your people took him and confiscated the money."

" Go to prison," promptly ordered the *Checka*. After that our friend was hauled up before them daily, and put through a species of Third Degree, but to all demands urged he could only make the same reply : " I did not send money to the White Army ! " At length the *Checka* determined to try other means of breaking down his will power. They ascertained that he was devotedly attached to his wife and his two children, so one day they said to him : " Your son is dying. Tell us the truth about the money and we will permit you to go home and see him."

The wretched man could only give the same answer as before—" I have told you the truth." He was sent back to prison, and his child died. But that was not the end of his torture. The Bolshevists had not yet finished their grim game with him. While he had been in prison his wife had been trying by every means within her power to effect his release. She had even gone to the length of offering bribes, but without result. Meanwhile, every day he was brought up before the *Checka* and subjected to the terrible mental torture of the Third Degree for hours on end, until at last the treatment drove him out of his mind. His wife was told of this final catastrophe, but did not relax her efforts to obtain his release. Mad or sane, she still loved and wanted her husband.

At length one day, an old family friend of theirs received the longed-for tidings that X—— was to be released. Sorrow was turned into joy, and there were the greatest rejoicings in that hitherto stricken household. The master was returning.

Next morning a telephone message came through : " X—— is released. *He has been shot!*" That was the *Checka's* idea of a jest. Such is Bolshevism. Small wonder indeed that those of us who have perforce bowed our necks beneath its bitter yoke will carry the scars to our dying day. Bolshevism and freedom! What a farce! It is a bondage beyond description. A slavery of spirit and body, which no pen can adequately describe.

CHAPTER 24

STORIES OF KINGS AND QUEENS I HAVE MET

A snub to Midas—The King of Sweden and the wealthy pork merchant—At the Sporting Club at Monte Carlo—The Duke of Manchester at the tables—The first time I danced before the Kaiser—His State visit to Petrograd—Petipa—A new ballet—An original chorus of ballerinas—Karsavina and I ruin the performance—The Kaiser admires our legs—In Berlin at the Kroll Theatre—I touch elbows with the German Emperor—My first meeting with King George and Queen Mary—A house party at Lord and Lady Fitzwilliam's—A story about the King—An Imperial Darby and Joan—The Prince of Wales—The most beautiful Grand Duchess at Court—The Ex-Queen of Greece—An Imperial Page is dismissed, and the reason — A Queen who lost her garter.

SOME people hold the mistaken opinion that money can buy them anything they want, and obtain an entrance for them anywhere. Personally, I always think this type of person is particularly objectionable, and am delighted if anybody has sufficient disrespect for Midas and his wiles to snub a worshipper. When I was at Monte Carlo one year I saw a delightful snub administered to a certain American millionaire who had amassed his dollars through pork, and was inclined to think that pork ruled the hemisphere.

My husband and I used to play baccarat at the Sporting Club with our friend the Grand Duke André, who was staying in Monte Carlo. Among other players was the King of Sweden. One evening we had all been playing together, and everybody had been losing with the exception of the pork merchant, who was waxing more impossible than ever in his jubilation over his victory. Nobody liked playing with him. But his unpopularity was not due to his rapacious capacity for winning, but because he showed everybody with such unpleasant plainness that he was under the impression that his dollars had bought the whole earth, including the club and all its members.

So far he had been unable to satisfy one great ambition, which was to become on speaking terms with the King of Sweden. Even his sublime audacity failed him at the thought of venturing to present himself, and as nobody would stand sponsor it looked as if he was doomed to disappointment. However, the brilliant idea occurred to him of playing until he had the chance of buying the bank. But it afforded a chance to get even with him which none of us could resist, for nobody covered his card. When this occurred three times in succession the infuriated pork merchant flung down his hand and strode out of the club. Let us hope he had at last assimilated the knowledge, bitter though it might be, that there are some things dollars cannot buy, among them being presentation to a king.

The Duke of Manchester often played at the tables when my husband and I were at Monte Carlo at that time. We found him a most interesting man. A mutual friend told us that he had inherited the outstanding personality of his mother, without her extreme bluntness. Possibly it was this latter quality that accounted for her being reputed to be " the only woman who was allowed to be rude to King Edward ! "

I have danced several times at Monte Carlo, and have always enjoyed my appearances there. Altogether I suppose that at some time or another I must have danced in most of the big capitals of Europe. The first occasion on which I danced before the Kaiser was in Russia and not Germany, however. It occurred when he was paying a State visit to the Tsar at St. Petersburg. A Gala performance was held in his honour at the Imperial Opera House. Great preparations were made for it, and our producer, Petipa, put on a new ballet, entitled " The Dance of the Shadows." Wishing to introduce something by way of a novelty he decided that the *Corps du Ballet* should be composed only of *première ballerinas*, and selected a number of principals to take these parts. Although his idea was an original one it was foredoomed to failure from the start because it was so utterly impracticable. To begin with, good team-work is essential for a first-class *Corps du Ballet*, and it is imperative, therefore, that each dancer should move simultaneously and with the precision of a squad of infantry. Now a *ballerina* can move at her own sweet will so long as she keeps within the *tempo* of the music, because she has only herself to consider, or at the utmost her dancing partner, who is trained usually to consider *her*, and to subordinate himself.

Petipa selected Karsavina and me to lead the two sections of the *Corps du Ballet* for " The Dance of the Shadows," but both of us were so unsuccessful as members of a chorus that after the Gala performance was over he flew into a violent passion with us and declared we had completely ruined the show. I came in for the brunt of the storm, and he raged at me—" As for you, you have too much personality for a *Corps du Ballet* altogether ! " Afterwards I comforted myself with the thought that this was really a backhanded fashion of advising me to go and become a *ballerina*. But at the time both Karsavina and I were extremely crestfallen. Our only consolation was the knowledge that we had satisfied the Imperial visitor. But then the Kaiser always had an eye for a gracefully shaped leg, and whatever Petipa might say about our movements, even he could find no possible fault with our legs !

The next time I saw the German Emperor was when I was in Berlin and had become transformed into a leading *ballerina*. I was dancing at the Kroll Theatre. One night when my dance was finished the management placed a box at my disposal, so my husband and I sat in it and watched the performance. This was a reversal of the usual situation which I found very enjoyable. The Kroll Theatre had been built in such a style that the boxes were adjacent to each other. When we took possession of our box there were no occupiers in the box next to it. In my eagerness to watch what was happening on the stage, I never perceived that my elbow was resting on the ledge of the adjoining box, nor did I hear its occupants arrive. My first intimation of their presence was when I felt somebody's elbow touching mine, and indignant at a stranger taking such a liberty with me turned round to see who it was. I found myself gazing into the eyes of the Kaiser, and awakened to the fact that it was the Imperial elbow that was guilty of seeking contact with mine.

The first occasion on which I danced before

KINGS AND QUEENS I HAVE MET 225

King George and Queen Mary occurred at a party given by Lord and Lady Fitzwilliam. Owing to their relationship with Mr. Fitzwilliam, a director of the Empire, arrangements were usually made for one or other of the stars there to perform at their private parties. They asked me to go down and stay at their country place for this particular party, and to organize a special entertainment as King George and Queen Mary were going to stay with them. I arranged an attractive programme, and everybody was very pleased. Afterwards Lady Fitzwilliam sent me a charming little brooch as a souvenir.

I was lately told the most delightful story concerning King George, which occurred during his recent illness. Queen Mary had been suffering from a cold, and had been obliged to keep to her own room. For three days she had been unable to visit the King. As soon as she was sufficiently recovered she hastened to his side, to be greeted with the words: "What a long time you have been away!"

"Only three days, George," protested Queen Mary, on which the King sighed, and murmured:

"Only three days! It seems more like *three weeks!*"

The first time I saw the Prince of Wales was when he was attending a big charity ball at Lansdowne House. Mr. Gordon Selfridge had lent the house and the Marchioness Curzon was organizing the ball. Most of my own countrymen are so tall that the Prince of Wales seemed quite short by comparison with them, but that did not prevent my copying the example set by all the other women, and falling in love with him.

On the opposite page is a photograph of me taken with Kschessinska's son, Count Krassinsky, when he was a small boy. I hear he is going to be married now and that his mother is opening a Ballet School in Paris. It is to be organized on the most up-to-date lines, and will possess its own swimming bath and manicure and beauty salons on the premises, where the pupils may cultivate beauty in the intervals of practising ballet steps. Still, after all, beauty and dancing are twin sisters, or should be, since one promotes the other and assists its growth.

One of the most beautiful of the younger Grand Duchesses at the Imperial Court was the one I have previously written about, the Grand Duchess Hélène, who is to-day the Ex-Queen of Greece. She has wonderful-looking eyes that are very large and dark. When she was a girl the Imperial pages were always delighted to find themselves allocated to her service, and did their best to fulfil all her wishes. But one day a new page got into serious trouble with his Imperial mistress who, although a beauty, was also an imperious one. I have already mentioned the fact that some boys of fourteen were men of the world in experience. The particular incident I am about to relate shows how their knowledge was sometimes increased. This new page was about seventeen years of age and by no means a man of the world, but on the contrary a very innocent lad. One day, to his great discomfiture, the Grand Duchess Hélène suddenly ordered him: "*My garter is too low! Arrange it for me!*"

Now it happened that she was in the habit of wearing her garters rather high. When the page

A Famous Dancer's Son.

Count Krassinsky, the son of the Grand Duke Serge and Kschessinska, the *ballerina*. With him in the garden is Madame Lydia Kyasht.

Facing page 226

timidly essayed to do her bidding his confusion was heightened still further by his being unable to locate it. Rumour hath it that he afterwards admitted he did not know where to look for a garter, and had never anticipated that looking for one would be one of his duties as an Imperial page. At any rate he failed to find it, and was promptly dismissed for neglecting to carry out his duties in a proper manner—which was an ironical way of putting it, to say the least of it!

CHAPTER 25

MY ESCAPE FROM RUSSIA

My three journeys to Russia to see my wounded husband—When he and Baron Engelhardt became privates in the British Army—Not expert potato peelers—At the Tsarskoe Palace during the revolution—On March 12th, 1917—The revolutionists surround the station at St. Petersburg—Our return to Tsarskoe Selo—Firing on the barracks there—A double-edged remark—Revolutionary methods of choosing officers—After six days—What the peasant said to the Tsar—The general demeanour of the army—Kerensky, the War Minister—In the Guard Room on the frontier—An historical document—The fortunes of war—" Only an old palace."

DURING the war I travelled three times to Russia in order to see my husband, who had been wounded and had many adventures when the revolution broke out, while I was trying to escape. My husband was a passenger on the last train that succeeded in getting through before the frontier was closed altogether to travellers, and had to disguise himself in order to achieve that feat. Afterwards he and his friend, Baron Engelhardt, joined the British Army as privates. One of the first tasks given them was to clean and peel potatoes for dinner. The regimental kitchen was situated about half a mile away, and the Sergeant ordered them to carry the tub full of peeled potatoes over there and give it to the Army cook. It was a most heavy and awkward utensil to carry. But they managed it somehow by means of wrapping their silk handkerchiefs round the handles.

MY ESCAPE FROM RUSSIA 229

When they arrived at the kitchen the cook gave one glance at the potatoes and exclaimed, "Do you call these clean? Take them away and do them again!" So my husband and his friend were obliged to tramp the half-mile back and inform the Sergeant. He was most indignant about it and promptly ordered them to return to the kitchen and insist on the cook's accepting the potatoes; so rather wearily this time Baron Engelhardt and Alexis tramped back again. Luck favoured them this time because it was nearly the dinner hour. The potatoes were in urgent demand and so the cook accepted them, with many cutting aspersions as to the poor culinary abilities of the two men.

When I was over in Russia I made an appeal at a Gala performance of the ballet for presents to give away to the English soldiers, and received quite a lot of money as well as thousands of boxes of cigarettes, all of which I brought back to England with me and distributed to the Tommies. I used to appeal also to English audiences. One night I collected over a hundred pounds from them, and purchased boots with it for the soldiers.

I was in Russia during the first days of the revolution, and was staying at the Tsarskoe Selo as my husband's regiment was stationed there. Our house stood a little apart from the others in the officers' quarters, and was subsequently in the thick of the revolution. I shall never forget March 12th, 1917, because it was the first day of the revolution. I was engaged to dance at the theatre in St. Petersburg, and went by train to the capital. Various people who met me on the way advised my turning back to Tsarskoe Selo, as they said revolution had broken out and people were being shot down on every side. I did not believe these stories, because everything had been so quiet in the barracks. But on arriving at St. Petersburg the station master informed me that the revolutionaries were already surrounding the station. All the women and children were taken into a side room for shelter, and the station master told us all that we should have to remain there until he could ascertain whether it would be safe to run us back in a train to Tsarskoe Selo. Naturally the principal aim of the revolutionaries was to prevent anybody returning to Tsarskoe Selo, as they knew that the garrison there was loyal to the Tsar and would do their best to quell any rising.

Meanwhile the street firing became fiercer and fiercer, and we could see some of the revolutionaries driving past in private motor-cars which they had commandeered, and firing at random on any passer-by. After we had waited for some while we were all put into a train and sent back to Tsarskoe Selo. We found everything was quiet there, and when I informed my husband and his brother officers that whole regiments in St. Petersburg had deserted and joined the revolutionaries they would not believe me. The next day more than proved the truth of my words, for the revolutionaries found their way to Tsarskoe Selo and began to fire on the barracks. Soon after this some officers from my husband's regiment came to my house and asked me to hide them. They thought, as our house was isolated from the rest, there would be less likelihood of their being discovered.

On the following morning the soldiers joined the revolutionaries and inaugurated their campaign by arresting all the officers with German sounding names, on the plea that "All our unhappiness comes from Germany!"—a remark which had a double-edged meaning and included the Tsarina as much as the officers. Any officers whom they liked were retained. As my husband did not meet with their disapproval they made him Commandant of the Military District of Tsarskoe Selo, and after a month promoted him to be the Colonel of the regiment. They chased the original Colonel and his senior officers out of the town.

It was surprising how soon all the excitement calmed down. Within six days from the first shot all the theatres and shops were open again and doing business, and the trams were running. But this was only the calm before the storm. A fortnight later the Tsar was arrested, and my husband's regiment, the First Rifle Guard, was placed in charge of him—an appalling position for the men among them who revered and loved him. The revolutionaries had promoted many peasants to the position of officers, and these had naturally no idea of military or court etiquette. One day when the Tsar was taking some exercise in the grounds, one of these young officers happened to be on guard. Seeing him standing there the Tsar came forward and extended his hand, but the uncouth youth put both his hands behind his back and said : "No, I will not give you my hands because when I was poor and *your* slave you did not come to help me. Now the situation is reversed, and I do not want to take *your* hand." The regular officers who were present were very much upset at this incident and at the idea of such an insult being offered to the man whom they still regarded as their Imperial ruler, but they dared do nothing openly to show their resentment.

There was a great difference noticeable in the general demeanour of the soldiers after the revolution. Prior to that all of them had been noted for their well-drilled ranks and their discipline. But later they were more notorious for squabbling and ill manners than for anything else. One day Kerensky, the War Minister, went to the front in order to review one of the regiments who did not want to fight. When he implored the men to do their best for the sake of their country they only laughed at him.

On my journey out of Russia I passed through the Guard Room at a frontier town, and saw a sheet of paper lying openly on the table, across which were written the words "Historical document." On inspection it proved to be a printed order with the date 1915 inscribed on it, and the Tsar's signature appended. It gave instructions for the arrest of Kerensky, describing him as a man who was a danger to the throne and who threatened its safety, and ordering him to be immediately sent to St. Petersburg to stand his trial. It was strange to think that only two years had elapsed, and that the man who was condemned in such a fashion had since become the Russian War Minister.

It took me a whole month before I succeeded in eventually reaching England and safety. I arrived in a state bordering on collapse.

Since those days mock battles have taken place in Petrograd instead of the real thing. When

Pudovkin, the Russian producer, was reproducing the scenes showing the bombardment of the Winter Palace in the film entitled "St. Petersburg," he used live shells. In order to give as realistic an effect as possible a gunboat was brought up the Neva and the Palace was shelled with four-inch guns, while a battery of field artillery was trained on it in front from the square. Pudovkin has very little Imperialistic sympathy about him. When somebody remonstrated with him concerning the damage he must have done, he merely remarked, "It was only one of the old palaces." The irony of it is that the film shelling is supposed to have done more damage than the real shelling in 1918. And so the palace of the Tsar—the scene of so many brilliant ceremonies—has become a location for film-making. Such is the harvest of revolution, and of the seeds sown by the Bolshevists!

CHAPTER 26

SOME ROYAL ROMANCES

What is romance?—Misinterpretations—How damsels of other centuries interpreted it—How modern women of to-day interpret it—Men are more romantic than women—A romantically inclined race—The Tsar as Don Quixote—His famous reply to Admiral Niloff—The Tsar's romantic attachment—His autocratic mistress—My retort to Kschessinska—Her marvellous home in Petrograd—Its Grecian bathroom and marble bath—Her parties and her Imperial guests—Where " gate-crashers " would be tabooed —The romance of the Grand Duke Serge and Kschessinska —His reputation—His generous gifts to his mistress— Sylvan lovers—The Grand Duke André admires me but falls in love with Kschessinska—Ballet performances in the Tsar's Camp—When I refused to obey the Imperial command—In disgrace—The Grand Duke Serge becomes a father—What the gossips said about it—Kschessinska'a little son and his wonderful toy—The Grand Duke Michael Milhailovitch—His general attitude towards life and his romance—The Grand Duke Serge is assassinated by the Bolshevists—Kschessinska's house is wrecked—A very different scene—A Christmas party at her home—I spoil a priceless lace tablecloth and am scolded by my hostess— " Her Imperial indignation "—How Kschessinska successfully converted enemies into friends—The Grand Duke Nicholas Nicholaievitch—His mistress Potozka—Their tragic romance—She seeks solace in drugs—Pearls and tears—A dramatic scene at the Grand Duke Boris's party —The victim of romance and the victor—An epicure of life—The rainbow of romance.

How dull life would become without any romance to brighten it. Romance is another word for love, and a word that is pathetically misinterpreted at times. Some people have actually gone so far as to apply the description of romantic to the life of Rasputin. A fitter title would be to call it an orgy of brutality and licentiousness. There is nothing in the least romantic about giving vent to one's feelings to the extent of behaving like a wild beast, and this was his mode of behaviour on certain occasions.

There seems to be a general lack of knowledge as to what really constitutes romance. This is surprising in an age when one is told "everything is known!" Quite a number of people still imagine that they are behaving romantically when they begin to fret and pine, and lose their appetite because their love affair has gone astray. We are told that in Victorian days young ladies suffered from the vapours, and exhibited signs of incipient consumption if they were jilted or were the victims of a dearth in proposals, and that the more tenacious carried it to the extent of fading altogether out of life. By this means they established a lifelong brand on the faithless swain, and made him a general object of remark and contumely, while retaining for themselves the more satisfactory reputation of a faithful heart. If anybody had possessed sufficient courage to call the action what it really was—a display of spite—the probability is that righteous indignation would have restored them to life to be a plague for ever after to their relations and friends.

Such episodes as these have recurred throughout the centuries. The Victorian age need not take the credit to itself of having the sole prerogative. For example, in Cromwell's time, when hearts were presumed to be "iron-clad," there were maidens in plenty who fell victims of unrequited love to sires of noble birth and lineage. The reason this does not happen so frequently in the present century is due, I think, to the fact that women have developed mentally and become broader minded. This transformation has been effected because conditions have compelled them to rub shoulders with mankind in order to provide the wherewithal to keep themselves. The result is that if any suffer a love disappointment necessity forces them to keep their brains so actively employed that they have no time left in which to sit down and brood over their errant swains.

On the whole I incline towards the opinion that men are more romantically disposed than women, and that this is the reason why some of them lose their heads over a woman when they themselves have reached an age when they should be thinking presumably of a future life and forswearing earthly pleasures. Very few men are humble enough to imagine themselves too old to make love to an attractive woman. She need not necessarily be a young girl, as sex appeal is not confined to the thirties, or the forties, or to any particular age. It is an inherent instinct that some women possess and always use, and that others never possess and never will. It is unteachable, as it is either inbred in a woman or else she has none.

Assuming that men are the more romantically inclined sex, may not that be the reason they are more successful in business ventures? The urge of romance and the void within themselves compel them to look elsewhere for a substitute. They are subconsciously seeking an outlet for their own sexual emotions, but of this fact they are unaware. They would probably be the first to laugh such a suggestion to scorn.

The Jews are at heart a romantically inclined race, but there is generally a tinge of melancholy about their romance, and they give one an impression of always seeking. They have never lost the sense of being a race set apart. This attitude has been engendered by their persecution through past centuries. Playwrights have held them up to ridicule. Shakespeare even did not spare them. He immortalized Shylock for the benefit of generations to come. Yet this is a portraiture of a single individual that should by no means be taken as typical of the whole race. One cannot judge a race by one individual. It would be unfair, for example, to condemn the Russians as a weak nation because their Tsar was a weak man. He was a Don Quixote, and suffered from an over-chivalrous complex which prevented him from taking a firm stand with the Tsarina and forcing her to submit to his will. His disposition was to take the line of least resistance in domestic affairs, as witness his well-known reply to Admiral Niloff when the latter implored him to rid the Court of Rasputin's evil presence. "*Better one Rasputin than ten hysterics!*" exclaimed the Tsar. This was an allusion in passing to the Tsarina's habit of indulging in violent hysterics whenever she was thwarted in any project she wished to carry through.

I have already mentioned the Tsar's previous romance with Kschessinska. She had such influence in the Imperial Ballet at that time that every whim of hers was granted the instant she expressed it. When Prince Volkonsky—the Director—ventured once to give her certain orders which did not meet with her approval, he was shortly afterwards dismissed. It became noised abroad in St. Petersburg that the favourite of the Emperor's son was responsible for this dismissal, and the people were so infuriated at her action that one night, when we were both appearing together in a ballet at the Imperial Opera House, they showed their displeasure in a practical form by applauding me vigorously and ignoring the *première ballerina*. Kschessinska flew into a violent rage about this, and asked me, " Are you buying the gallery to applaud you ? " My answer did not tend to pour any oil on the troubled waters, for I retorted, " Since I have only five pounds a month salary, how can I buy the gallery ? " She reigned as queen in those days over St. Petersburg's artistic circles, and as she never permitted anybody but herself to have an acknowledged success on the stage, it was not surprising she should have become angry with the audience for daring to applaud me. We were destined to become friends later.

Kschessinska was very wealthy and built herself a marvellous house. It cost over a million roubles, and was constructed after the style of a French villa. It was situated immediately opposite the Winter Palace, where the Tsar resided when he was in the capital. The interior was furnished in the modern period. She followed the example set by the Grand Duke Boris, and chose English furniture. Her dining-room was furnished in fumed oak, which was very popular at that time in England. She was especially proud of her bathroom. It resembled a Grecian bathing pool, as the bath itself was made of white marble and sunk in the floor. The walls were white marble inlaid with blue and silver mosaic. Transparent net curtains were hung round the sunken bath, which gave a bather the impression of gazing through a limitless blue vista. All the fittings and furniture corresponded, while a rich blue and silver carpet covered the entire floor.

Kschessinska held parties in her bathroom, and we all sat there and smoked and talked. She was a wonderful hostess and her parties were very popular. The Tsar never came to any, but all the younger Grand Dukes, including Boris, Prince Gabriel, Prince Igor, and André, as well as the Grand Duke Serge Milhailovitch, whose father was a great-uncle of the Tsar, a son of the Emperor Nicholas the First, were to be met there. The principal reason everybody enjoyed Kschessinska's parties was because a general feeling of informality and goodwill prevailed. I think the reason this spirit was so prominent was because formal parties were not as fashionable in Russia as in England and America. The majority of Russians preferred to keep to intimate parties where the guests were personal friends, and chosen moreover because their hostess wanted to see them and liked them. Nobody would have dreamt of turning their house into a free hotel and providing free entertainments for persons they had never seen before in their lives, and probably never wished to see again. "Gate-crashers" would have had but a poor chance of obtaining any free hospitality in Russia.

Kschessinska used to be a great gambler at one time and was very fond of playing poker. I remember once at Monte Carlo she lost two million francs at the tables. After the marriage of the Tsar the beautiful *ballerina* came under the protection of the Grand Duke Serge. This astonished many people who had always regarded him as a very serious-minded man, and not at all inclined to form a romantic attachment for anybody, least of all someone outside the Imperial circle. He was a bachelor, and reputed to be the tallest man in Russia. The chief feature I remember about him were his eyes, because they were such an unusually warm blue in colouring and held the kindliest expression in their depths. As far as he was concerned the world was peopled by one woman after he met Kschessinska, and he belonged to her body and soul. It was not merely a physical union with him, but an absolute mating of everything. They were officially acknowledged to be lovers. It was common report that he had provided the money with which to build her wonderful house in St. Petersburg. She named it Kschessinska House, and when a big competition was organized by some of the leading Russian architects to discover the best-built house, hers won the prize. This greatly elated her. When the revolution broke out Lenin seized Kschessinska House and made it his headquarters.

The Grand Duke Serge gave her also a marvellous summer residence at Strelina, which is about thirty miles outside St. Petersburg. The grounds sloped down to the seashore. A beautiful forest surrounded the property, and the Grand Duke had it planted thickly with mushrooms because Kschessinska loved to gather them. Every morning the lovers wandered into the forest and

SOME ROYAL ROMANCES

returned laden with mushrooms. These are a favourite delicacy in Russia. We eat the species that English people consider poisonous, and have them cooked in butter and cream, and served chopped up into small pieces.

The Grand Duke André was yet another of the Imperial Princes who fell a victim to Kschessinska. I think that must have been a reason for my unpopularity with her at first, because he then admired me, and she was not the type of woman to tolerate any divided admiration.

When the Tsar went into camp special performances of the ballet were given there at his private theatre. This was only opened during the summer months and remained closed for the rest of the year. It accommodated comfortably about eight hundred persons. Only officers of the Imperial Guards were permitted to attend performances. They each had to pay for the privilege of admission and the tickets were expensive. The first seven rows of stalls, which were priced at sixteen shillings each, were reserved for the senior officers, and nobody below a Colonel in rank was allowed to occupy one. The rule that all junior officers must stand during an interval was reinforced here to include all officers, and the audience had to either stand for the whole of the ten minutes' interval, or else remain outside in the foyer.

One evening when I was dancing there the Grand Duke André was present. During the interval he invited me to take supper with him after the performance, but I told him that I had a previous engagement. " With whom ? " he demanded, and when I explained that I had promised to have supper with Alexis, he exclaimed angrily, "Ragosin again! If you do not come with me, I will never pardon you!"

When the ballet was ended he sent his Aide-de-Camp to fetch me, but I refused to go. There was a terrible row the next day over my boldness in daring to disobey the Grand Duke's command, and I was in great disgrace for some time. When the Grand Duke André became enamoured later of Kschessinska he had eyes for nobody else, and after her little son was born some people were unkind enough to suggest that although Serge was the official father the baby was the exact image of André. They talked all the more when it was known that the Grand Duke Vladimir, André's father, had consented to be godfather to the baby. The latter was very devoted to his little godson, and made him a present of a wonderful doll's house that was large enough to accommodate himself and some of his playfellows. It was built in the grounds of the country house at Strelina, and was the most perfect model in miniature of a house I have ever seen, as, besides containing the usual reception rooms, it possessed a kitchen and bathroom, and a fascinating staircase that the children could ascend and descend at their pleasure.

Kschessinska adores her son, Count Vladimir Krassinsky, and has spoilt him terribly. His father, the Grand Duke Serge, was likewise very devoted to him. I remember one day when I went into the nursery I found him kneeling beside the child's cot, and listening with the most rapt attention while the little fellow lisped forth his baby prayers. That picture of the father and son will linger long in my memory.

SOME ROYAL ROMANCES 243

I have previously mentioned his brother, the Grand Duke Michael Milhailovitch, who resided at Kenwood in England for so many years. He contracted a morganatic marriage with the Countess Torby, who was the morganatic daughter of Prince Nicholas of Nassau. The two brothers had one thing in common : having bestowed their heart on one woman nothing could alter their affection ; for, although the Grand Duke Michael was forbidden to marry the girl he loved, he steadfastly refused to obey the Imperial decree and chose banishment in preference. I think his general attitude towards life is best summed up in his own words : "*Which is the greatest happiness in this world ? Surely love for a woman—the choice of our future life!*"

His two daughters married, it will be remembered, and became subsequently the Marchioness of Milford Haven and Lady Zia Wernher.

The Grand Duke Serge was assassinated by the Bolshevists in 1918. But previous to his death Kschessinska was already homeless, and Lenin could be seen standing on the balcony of her house. From this vantage he would address the people gathered below in the street, and would incite them with all the oratory at his command to loot and murder where they had previously bowed the knee. Kschessinska did not fear the fury of the mob for herself, but undoubtedly she dreaded the thought that they might harm her cherished son. She preferred to leave her home to their mercy and take her son into safety instead of remaining to defend her property. The mob took full advantage of the opportunity afforded by her absence. They ransacked the beautiful house from top to bottom and left it an uninhabitable shell, with shattered windows and broken doors.

When I heard what had happened I could not help thinking of a very different scene there. Kschessinska had issued invitations to her friends to come to a Christmas party, and as I happened to be paying one of my brief visits to St. Petersburg I received an invitation. The dinner table was a wonderful spectacle, spread with gold plate and antique glass. She had just been given a present of a valuable lace tablecloth which she was using for the first time that evening. When we all sat down to dinner she warned us : " Now take great care not to spill any of the red wine on my new lace cloth. If you do you will spoil it, and it is a very valuable piece of lace. Lydia is especially to be careful ! " she added, knowing from past experience my fatal propensity for getting into mischief.

I was so nervous that I implored no wine should be given me. But Kschessinska would not hear of my going without, and said everybody must drink her health. In a weak moment I yielded. Of course, with my usual ill luck, somebody jogged my elbow, and the entire contents of my wine glass were spilt over my hostess's priceless lace cloth. Kschessinska was very angry indeed with me, and I felt most miserable. Her scoldings were usually delivered in such a charming fashion that the culprit rather enjoyed them than otherwise, always supposing, that is, that she was not indulging in what the ballet termed " *Her Imperial indignation !* " As a matter of fact, in spite of the fact that she was extremely quick-tempered and prone to take offence at trifles, she possessed very few enemies, and those she had, once they met her, were speedily converted into friends. Personally, I think even the notorious Lenin would have succumbed to her charms, and presented her with her own house if he had met and talked to her before first taking possession.

I have previously mentioned the Grand Duke Nicholas Nicholaievitch. His marriage with the Princess Anastasia was one of the most tragic Royal marriages of convenience that I know about. He was fifty years of age when it took place, and had been living for over twenty years with the Russian actress Potozka. She adored him, and when he left and broke off their intimate relationship she was so desperate that she took to drugs in a vain attempt to forget her grief and stifle the pangs of memory. He had been a very generous lover, and gave her some wonderful jewels, including a rope of pearls that was supposed to be one of the finest in Russia, and which she wore constantly. Whether the superstition that pearls bring tears is true or not, it is a certain fact that these particular pearls brought tears to Potozka.

One evening after the Grand Duke Nicholas's marriage had taken place, I went to a party at Boris's villa and found Potozka was one of the guests. She was in her then usual condition of being half stupefied by drugs. Her presence seemed to cast a gloom somehow over the party, and none of us were as merry as usual. We were making our farewells to Boris and thanking him for his hospitality when Potozka slowly descended the wide staircase. She looked terribly unhappy. Midway she paused and seemed to be seized with an absolute frenzy of despair. As we watched her she tore at the precious pearls wound round and round her throat, as if they were choking her, and broke the rope in half. The precious beads scattered in all directions. Some of them rolled down the stairs and fell into the lounge hall below. Instead of finishing our farewells to our host we all rushed back, and going down on our hands and knees instituted a frantic search. Meanwhile Potozka, the author of all the pother, stood immovable as a rock on the staircase. She was apparently lost in thought and did not trouble in the least whether her pearls were found or not. From her point of view the only thing that mattered was the fact that she had been supplanted, and that her Imperial lover had obeyed the dictates of state and left her. Perhaps if she had given him a child he would not have done so. She is still alive, but I do not know what she is doing. Undoubtedly the tragic ending to her love affair cast a blight over her life.

During the war the Grand Duke Nicholas commanded the Russian Armies. He was one of the group who advised the Tsar to abdicate, even going so far as to state that it was the only thing for the Emperor to do. He escaped from Russia, and died in 1928 in the South of France. He was very much mourned by all Russians who were loyal in their hearts to the Imperial régime.

Potozka was the victim of romance, whereas Kschessinska was the victor and enjoyed to the full all the fruits of her victories. Yet each of them tasted of the fount of life in her own way, and learnt to appreciate it from a different angle to those who have never experienced the combined joy and sorrow of romance. If one judges both from a dispassionate angle one must grant that Potozka was of a very passionate disposition, and temperamentally inclined to take tragedy hard. Moreover, her association with her Imperial lover had lasted for so many years that she had begun to feel less of a mistress and more of a wife. Hers was not the nature that could seek and find solace in the arms of a fresh lover. As far as she herself was concerned, romance began and ended with one man.

The Russian is an epicure of life, and quite unconsciously the famous French writer Rousseau gave a very accurate summing-up of his character when he wrote that "*The man who has lived the most is not he who can count the most years, but he who has most appreciated life.*" Many of Rousseau's writings display an intimate knowledge of the passionate side of life, as well as of romance. My own country people have absorbed the doctrine he advocated that only those live the most who have appreciated life at its fullest. They show their gratitude by living every second of the span that the Great Weaver of all has allotted them. To them life is as it is to myself, a rainbow. Its glorified tints of love and passion colour the daily drops of rain until they become transformed, and illumined by a radiance that never fades but remains for ever as a beatified memory of romance.

FINIS

www.ingramcontent.com/pod-product-compliance
Lightning Source LLC
Chambersburg PA
CBHW071224080526
44587CB00013BA/1496